Series / Number 02-034

Coalitions and Future War:
A Dyadic Study of
Cooperation and Conflict

HARVEY STARR
Indiana University

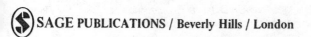 SAGE PUBLICATIONS / Beverly Hills / London

For information address:

SAGE PUBLICATIONS, INC.
275 South Beverly Drive
Beverly Hills, California 90212

SAGE PUBLICATIONS LTD
St George's House / 44 Hatton Garden
London EC1N 8ER

International Standard Book Number 0-8039-0524-6

Library of Congress Catalog Card No. 74-27553

FIRST PRINTING

When citing a professional paper, please use the proper form. Remember to cite the correct Sage Professional Paper series title and include the paper number. One of the two following formats can be adapted (depending on the style manual used):

(1) AZAR, E. E. (1972) "International Events Interaction Analysis." Sage Professional Papers in International Studies, 1, 02-001. Beverly Hills and London: Sage Pubns.

OR

(2) Azar, Edward E. 1972. *International Events Interaction Analysis.* Sage Professional Papers in International Studies, vol. 1, series no. 02-001. Beverly Hills and London: Sage Publications.

CONTENTS

Coalitions and Future War:
A Dyadic Study of
Cooperation and Conflict

HARVEY STARR
Indiana University

INTRODUCTION: GENERAL AND
SPECIFIC CONCERNS

"War, to be abolished, must be understood. To be understood, it must be studied" (Karl Deutsch, 1964: xii). Indeed, it has been noted that, "Students of war are under a special injunction to 'publish or perish'" (Hanson and Russett, 1972: 9). In step with these sentiments, there has been within the last few years a burgeoning literature concerned with the causes and correlates of war.[1] This literature, empirical and quantitative in nature, has dealt with a wide variety of variables: attributes of the international system, attributes of the international actors, behavioral outputs of these actors, the previous nature of both attributes and behavior. This study wishes to look at war itself as a "previous" experience; to view one type of previous war experience as a correlate (and perhaps cause) of subsequent war behavior.

It must be made clear, however, that the war experience per se is not the focus of the present study, but a more specific type of war experience: the war coalition experience. Thus we will not be looking at war

AUTHOR'S NOTE: *I would like to acknowledge the support provided to me for this research by Indiana University in the form of a 1973 Summer Faculty Research Fellowship. I would like also to thank the Indiana University Department of Political Science Data Laboratory, and its Director, Professor Ron Weber, for the use of its facilities and its aid in preparation of data. Expressions of appreciation are also due to Dina Zinnes, Frank Hoole, Brian Job, Ben Most, and the two anonymous reviewers, for their comments on various earlier drafts. Of course, all analysis, interpretation, and errors are my own responsibility.*

participation in general—all nations which have engaged in war—but <u>that</u> <u>subset of warring nations</u> that have participated in war coalitions. The war coalition experience provides an interplay of two phenomena: the cooperative coalition experience and the belligerent experience of being at war. In terms of all possible dyads in the international system, the dyads upon which this study will focus are those in which the two nations have been members of war coalitions: nations which have cooperated in war, at the expense of blood and treasure, to fight against some common foe.

In essence, the specific question to be addressed in this study is how an experience affects those taking part in that experience. The specific experience under consideration is that of fighting in a war coalition. The two basic questions are:

(1) Does war coalition partnership have an impact on the choice of future war allies and war enemies?

(2) What factors, characteristics, or attributes of the war coalition or the dyad of war coalition partners, are related to the future choice of war coalition partners as allies or enemies?

In sum, we wish first to look for patterns of future war behavior for war coalition participants. If such patterns emerge, we then wish to investigate a further set of secondary variables to help explain the patterns in more detail.[2]

The above outlines the specific concerns of this research. However, in addressing these concerns we must confront the broader context and the broader implications involved in such a study. First, this study addresses the important question of *consequences* of war. That is, what sorts of things result from the activity that is war? In this study we wish to investigate how a war coalition experience affects future war behavior; how one type of war experience affects future ones. While the author has previously studied the consequences of war in terms of the distribution of payoffs among war coalition partners (Starr, 1972), scholars in general are only slowly coming to the study of the things that wars cause. Such study means, in effect, looking at the phenomenon of war itself as an independent variable, and building feedback loops into the study of war.

A related literature, but more developed, has to do with war termination. Students of war termination recognize, as does the present study, that there are both interesting and important questions to be investigated after war has broken out, and indeed, after hostilities have ended. Berenice Carroll (1969: 296) has developed five categories of questions those studying war termination should attempt to answer. These include a concern with, "Evaluative questions concerning war outcomes or peace settlements and their *consequences* for post-war conditions, preservation of peace, *changes* in the international system, and *options for the future*" (italics added). In looking at the relationship between the war coalition experience of nations and their subsequent behavior, we hope to begin to answer these types of questions.

In addition, the present study continues the earlier effort to link one of the major cooperative activities of international relations (alliance or alignment) to the central conflictual activity (war). The association of cooperation to future conflict and cooperation is an important focus of research, and has prompted attention by international relations scholars, though probably too few. Focusing on the war coalition as the cooperative activity, this study continues the investigation of questions concerning the effects of cooperation extant in both the alliance literature, and in the literature on international integration. Here we also begin to look at possible evidence concerning "learning" in international relations—learning habits of cooperation—as well as looking at "forgetting," in terms of the time between the war coalition and the next subsequent war experience of the war coalition partners.

Finally, looking ahead to the second of the questions listed above concerning the characteristics and attributes of war coalition dyads, we will be developing new evidence about the roles of two major factors found in the study-of-war literature: the role of major powers and major power status; and the role of contiguity in both the choice of war opponents and in the probability of going to war. Major power status and contiguity are both, in turn, associated with the role and importance of increased interactions in international relations, and how increasing or decreasing interactions affect the cooperative and conflictual behavior of nations.

These few paragraphs hopefully will serve to alert the reader to some of the broader questions forming the context to the present, more specific, research. The focus here is systemic and macro-quantitative, with the dyad as the unit of investigation. The questions involve how previous behavior relates to later behavior. To these concerns we now turn.

PREVIOUS EXPERIENCE AS A BEHAVIORAL INPUT

The question of previous cooperation as an influence on future cooperation and conflict behavior is not a new one. Lewis Fry Richardson, in his pioneering *Statistics of Deadly Quarrels* investigated the effects of alliances and "comradeship in war." He asked, "Does alliance in war bind nations together?" (Richardson, 1960: 194) He concluded that wartime alliances did appear to have a pacifying effect, checking somewhat the incidence of war between former war alliance partners. This pacifying effect, Richardson claimed, was one that declined over time. Looking at previous activity more broadly, J. David Singer, in designing the long-term Correlates of War project has indicated plans to include feedback loops, "so that war will serve as a predictor as well as an outcome variable," reflecting the belief that war has a considerable impact on the system in which it takes place (Singer, 1972: 253).

How or why should previous war experience affect subsequent experiences? Drawing an analogy from interpersonal behavior, we note that laboratory research by psychologists has demonstrated that new hostility is often displaced on objects upon which past hostility is already felt. It may be proposed that traditions of past conflict will heighten the probability of future conflict (see Pruitt and Snyder, 1969: 29-30). Conversely, we may assume some positive impact from the bonds of cooperation and the habits of cooperation may be influenced by those of the past.

Dean Pruitt and Richard Snyder note (1969: 178): "Cooperation between states can engender friendly feelings among their citizens that later act to inhibit the use of violence." In part, the relationship between past and future cooperation has been tested by Roger Cobb and Charles Elder in their study of international integration. Drawing from the work of Etzioni, Galtung, Ernst Haas, Teune, and "socio-psychological learning mechanisms" models, they propose (1970: 48): "Nations will be more likely to develop attitudinal and transactional ties if they have collaborated previously." Past cooperative behavior, it is proposed, promotes "mutual relevance" between people and aids in future cooperative activity. They conclude, after analysis by canonical correlation, that "prior collaborative experience and wartime alignments do tend to predict to ensuing transactional exchange," (1970: 119-121) which is the best predictor of future cooperative behavior. Similarly, in a study of informal international alignments, John D. Sullivan, using the dyad as unit of analysis, has found that past intensity of alignment and past scope of alignment are strongly related to future intensity and scope of alignment (Sullivan, 1972: 127-129).

Based on the material briefly reviewed above we may now propose a working hypothesis. This hypothesis proposes that war coalition partners will comprise dyads that in future mutual war involvement are more likely to be allies and much less likely to be enemies. In testing this hypothesis we will also be testing the assumption that the war coalition experience is important and "unique." If the war coalition experience, as will be tested below, does not produce future patterns of behavior different from other contemporary and comparable forms of experience then we should not be focusing on war coalitions but upon some other, broader, experience. The assumption, implicit so far, is that the war coalition, as a form of international cooperation, is in some way a unique experience. Thus, in testing the above hypotheses we are testing two things: that war coalitions produce a special type of international experience; and that this experience is unique by producing future patterns of war involvement which tend heavily towards continued allied behavior. In the next section the data base will be set forth, key concepts will be operationalized, and the above hypothesis will be tested.

FUTURE WAR BEHAVIOR:
THE WAR COALITION PARTNERSHIP EXPERIENCE

The notion of war coalition experience will be operationalized by data collected in the author's earlier study (Starr, 1972).[3] In that study 36 war coalitions which took part in wars that occurred between 1821 and 1967 were delineated. These 36 coalitions contained 172 war coalition partners. The partners *within* each coalition—those who shared the experience of cooperating at war—make up the data base from which the dyads to be analyzed here were created. Each of the war coalitions was taken separately, and all possible dyads were derived: $n(n-1)/2$. This procedure yielded a total of 624 War Coalition Participant dyads—those dyads composed of two nations which shared a common war coalition experience.

The notion of future war behavior will be operationalized by the occurrence in time of the *next mutual war experience* of the dyad. For each dyad we have proceeded through history to locate the next *mutual* war experience: the very first time in history after the conclusion of the war in which the war coalition took part (and from which the dyad was derived), that the pair of war coalition partners (the dyad) were mutually involved in another war. The next mutual war experience will be abbreviated by the term Nextwar. The cutoff date for possible Nextwars was set at 1972. Finally, it should be noted that because we are interested in the consequences of a specific experience—a war coalition—we focus on the next possible occurrence of that event. The question of causes and influences on war, with its multitude of intervening variables, is sufficiently complex without attempting to take the analysis beyond the next involvement in war. In effect it is being proposed that this study will confirm a process similar to a first order Markov process. This will be discussed further below.

Admittedly, part of this definition of a Nextwar is open ended—the length of time between the war coalition and the occurrence of a next mutual war involvement. As noted, part of this research will deal with aspects of "learning" and "forgetting" in international relations. The main concern will be merely that of one experience relating to a subsequent experience. However, in sections below which discuss various hypotheses and explanatory variables, and in the data analysis section, we will indeed look at the impact of this timespan between war experiences. The sample of dyads to be analyzed will be divided into groups composed of those dyads formed less than and more than 25 years since the war coalition. As developed more fully below, this split relates to research dealing with possible generational effects in international cycles of conflict, and Richardson's notions of declining cooperative effects over time. Let us merely note here that only 15.5% of the dyads under analysis in those sections form at a point longer than 25 years from the war coalition, and that the most relevant statistical associations concern those dyads formed within 25 years of the war coalition.

To summarize, at some prior time 't' there exists a war coalition. From this coalition all possible dyads are derived. For *each* dyad, history is scanned to find the *next* time in history that the nations in that dyad are both involved again in the same war. The war coalition is at 't'; the Nextwar is at some 't+k' (with 'k' a variable length of time). To continue, at 't+k' there are only three possible configurations for the dyad. The two nations in the dyad may be Allies once more; they may have switched and become Enemies; or there may not be any Nextwar. That is, the two nations in the dyad may never again in history become involved in the same war. In that case the dyad may be labelled at 't+k' as NI (never involved again); see Table 1.

We have thus labelled the three possible types of future dyads, those at 't+k'. There are also three types of dyads at 't' which we must deal with. These are used to operationalize and test the notion that the war coalition experience is different from alternative experiences. Since this research is focused on the war coalition, the idea of war coalition experience, as noted, may be operationalized by War Coalition Participant dyads. These were discussed above as all the possible dyads which can be created from the members of any particular war coalition. Again, this produces a total of 624 War Coalition Participant dyads (see Table 3).

TABLE 1
Types of Dyads

At 't'

War Coalition
Participant Dyads:

all possible dyadic combinations of the
nations within any one war coalition;
these are then totalled for all coalitions

Belligerent Dyads:

all possible dyadic combinations of the
nations within a specific war coalition
and its opponent(s) during that war; these
are then totalled for all coalitions

Non-Participant Dyads:

all possible dyadic combinations of the
nations within a specific war coalition
and the members of the international
system at that time not participating in
that war; these are then totalled for all
coalitions

EXAMPLE:

War Coalition (A,B,C,) vs. Opponent (D)*
Non-Participant system members (E,F,G,H,I)

War Coalition
Participant Dyads: AB,AC,BC

Belligerent Dyads: AD,BD,CD

Non-Participant Dyads: EA,EB,EC,FA,FB,FC,GA,GB,GC,
                                   HA,HB,HC,IA,IB,IC

At 't+k'

In terms of future war relationships these dyads may be coded--

Allies: once more war coalition partners

Enemies: a switch to war opponents

NI: never become involved again together in war

---

* There is only one coalition in this war, A, B, C. Because D is not a member of a
coalition, it is not used to form dyads with Non-Participant system members. If D
were in a coalition, say D, X, Z, three more War Coalition Participant dyads, six more
Belligerent dyads and 10 more Non-Participant dyads would be created.

With what may we compare the War Coalition Participant dyads?
Keeping in mind that we are concerned with the war coalition experience,
we must find comparisons which cover all the possible international
relationships that a war coalition partner might have *at the time of his*

involvement in the war coalition. There are, as noted, only three possibilities. A war coalition participant may comprise a dyad with one of his war coalition partners: War Coalition Participant dyads. A war coalition participant may also combine in a dyad with the (or an) opponent which is fighting against the war coalition. Thus a second type of 't' dyad may be called a Belligerent dyad. For each war coalition, all the war coalition partners were taken and combined into all possible dyads with the nation(s) they were fighting in *that* war. Having done so for all coalitions, the results were summed, providing a total of 342 Belligerent dyads.

There is one final possibility for a war coalition participant. During any war in history, in addition to one's partners and opponents, there are a number of nations in the international system that are *not participating in that war.* These are the bystanders in the international system that occur with every war. A war coalition partner may thus also combine to form a dyad with one of these nations that are not participating in the war in which the war coalition is involved. This third type of 't' dyad may be called a Non-Participant dyad. For each war coalition, all war coalition partners were taken and used to comprise all possible dyads with those nations in the international system not participating in the war. Having done so for all war coalitions, the results were summed, providing a total of 3,040 Non-Participant dyads.[4]

Table 1 summarizes the three possible types of dyads at time 't'. A careful look at the labels for these dyads shows that they reflect the status of the "second" nation in the dyad. One nation in the dyad will *always* be a member of a war coalition. The other nation may then be either a war coalition partner (War Coalition Participant dyad), an opponent (Belligerent dyad), or a member of the international system not participating in this particular war (Non-Participant dyad). With these three types of dyads we can compare the war coalition experiences of nations to the other possible experiences the same nations could have had with non-war coalition partners. Table 1 also summarizes the three possible 't+k' relationships: Allies, Enemies, NI (never involved).

One historical example will suffice to illustrate our six different types of dyads. A simple illustration is the Schleswig-Holstein War of 1864. In this war a coalition was involved: Austria and Prussia (the simplest kind, two members). The opponent was Denmark; and according to the data provided by Singer and Small (1966a), there were 36 other national units that met their criteria for inclusion in the international system at the end of the war—units which did not participate in the war.

Thus, there is only one War Coalition Participant dyad, Austria/Prussia; there were two Belligerent dyads, Austria/Denmark and Prussia/Denmark;

and there were 72 Non-Participant dyads, Austria and each of the 36 non-participating system members, and Prussia and each of the 36 non-participating system members. All together this war coalition experience created 75 't' dyads. Starting in 1865 we now look forward in time to see how the Nextwar for each dyad shall be coded. Austria/Prussia will be coded as Allies, for the next time both states appear in the same war they are again partners, in 1900 during the Boxer Rebellion. Prussia/Denmark is coded Enemies, as the next time they appear in war together is World War II, once again on opposite sides. Austria/Denmark is coded NI (never involved in the future) as Austria and Denmark fail to become mutually involved in war again in the future. This same procedure is followed for each of the 72 dyads involving Austria and Prussia with the system non-participants.

Our working hypothesis may now be refined. We may propose that War Coalition Participant dyads will produce 't+k' patterns that are unique— that are statistically different from the patterns produced by Belligerent dyads and Non-Participant dyads. Moreover, War Coalition Participant dyads will be more likely to become Allies at 't+k', and less likely to become Enemies at 't+k' than Belligerent dyads or Non-Participant dyads. These relationships may be seen more clearly in Table 2. The letters in that table represent the *number* of dyads in any given category. The hypothesized relationships discussed above are represented symbolically using letters and mathematical notation.

Table 3 provides the frequencies of the types of dyads at periods 't' and 't+k', and are set up in such a way as to allow us to begin to test our hypotheses. In Table 2, the relationships set out under (a) propose that War Coalition Participant dyads patterns will be different from the other two patterns. Both parts of Table 3 confirm this, with the chi-square used to test the differences in over-all patterns. These differences are statistically quite significant.[5]

Moreover, the table permits us to posit that there is at work a process much like a first order Markov process. This is important, as we can conceive of the Markov process as an implicit predictive model which sets boundaries around the probabilities of future events or "states;" a process which indicates the transitional probabilities from one "state" to another. The periods 't' and 't+k' may be viewed as two such separate states or trials, with the second depending on the first. Simply, the probability of something occurring at 't+k' is assumed to be based on what has occurred at 't'.[6] As both parts of Table 3 demonstrate, what occurs at 't+k' does appear to be related to distinct patterns of occurence at 't'. Looking at Part A, simply viewing the percentages, we see that allies at 't', War

TABLE 2
A Symbolic Representation of Hypothesis 1:
The Relationship Between 't' and 't+k' Dyads*

		't+k'		
		<u>Allies</u>	<u>Enemies</u>	<u>NI</u>
't'	War Coalition ⟶ Participant Dyads	L	M	N
	Belligerent Dyads ⟶	Q	R	S
	Non-Participant Dyads ⟶	X	Y	Z

Hypothesis 1: War Coalition Participant dyads are 'unique'

(a) $LMN \neq QRS$
$LMN \neq XYZ$

War Coalition Participant dyads are more likely to be Allies and less likely to be Enemies

(b)   (c)

$$\frac{L}{L+M+N} > \frac{Q}{Q+R+S} \qquad : \qquad \frac{L}{L+M} > \frac{Q}{Q+R}$$

$$\frac{L}{L+M+N} > \frac{X}{X+Y+Z} \qquad : \qquad \frac{L}{L+M} > \frac{X}{X+Y}$$

$$\frac{M}{L+M+N} < \frac{R}{Q+R+S} \qquad : \qquad \frac{M}{L+M} < \frac{R}{Q+R}$$

$$\frac{M}{L+M+N} < \frac{Y}{X+Y+Z} \qquad : \qquad \frac{M}{L+M} < \frac{Y}{X+Y}$$

* Letters stand for numbers of dyads.

Coalition Participant dyads, produce the highest percentage of Allies at 't+k' (34% against 18% and 9%). Opponents at 't', the Belligerent dyads, produce the highest percentage of Enemies at 't+k' (19% to 13.5% and 6%). Similarly, the uninvolved at 't', the Non-Participant dyads, produce the highest percentage of dyads which never become involved again in the

TABLE 3
Dyadic Patterns of Future War Involvement

Part A. All Dyads

		't+k'				
		Allies	Enemies	NI	Total	
	War Coalition Participant Dyads	213 (34.1%)	84 (13.5%)	327 (52.4%)	624	(100%)
't'	Belligerent Dyads	61 (17.8%)	66 (19.3%)	215 (62.0%)	342	(100%)
	Non-Participant Dyads	262 (8.6%)	172 (5.7%)	2606 (85.7%)	3040	(100%)
		536	322	3148	4006	

x^2 = 440.26
df = 4
prob. = < .001

Part B. 'Involved' Dyads Only at 't+k'

		't+k'			
		Allies	Enemies	Total	
	War Coalition Participant Dyads	213 71.7%	84 28.3%	297	
't'	Belligerent Dyads	61 48.0%	66 52.0%	127	
	Non-Participant Dyads	262 60.4%	172 39.6%	434	
		536	322	858	

x^2 = 22.7
df = 2
prob. = <.001

future (86% to 62% and 52%). Borrowing the notation used by Wilkenfeld (1972: 283) we are saying in effect that: $D_t \rightarrow D_{t+k}$, where D refers to the type of dyad.

Looking to Part B, where only the "involved" dyads are set out—those dyads in which there was future war behavior—the first two patterns are reinforced. War Coalition Participant dyads produce the highest percentage of Allies at 't+k', while Belligerent dyads produce the highest percentage of Enemies.

The data discussed in Table 3, however, only starts us on our way to confirming the relationships set out in sections (b) and (c) of Table 2. In

TABLE 4
War Coalition Participant Dyads
Compared to Belligerent Dyads

Part A.

		't+k'			
		Allies	Enemies	NI	Total
't'	War Coalition Participant Dyads	213	84	327	624
	Belligerent Dyads	61	66	215	342
		274	150	542	966

x^2 = 29.8
df = 2
prob. = .001

Part B. 't+k' Comparisons: All Dyads

	't+k'		
	Allies	Enemies	NI
War Coalition Participant Dyads	34.1%	13.5%	52.4%
Belligerent Dyads	17.8%	19.3%	62.8%
	Z=5.4 prob.=.0001	Z=2.38 prob.=.009	Z=3.12 prob.=.0009

Part C. 't+k' Comparisons: Involved Dyads Only

	't+k'	
	Allies	Enemies
War Coalition Participant Dyads	72%	28%
Belligerent Dyads	48%	52%
	Z=4.74 prob.=.0001	Z=4.55 prob.=.0001

TABLE 5
War Coalition Participant Dyads
Compared to Non-Participant Dyads

Part A.

	't+k'			
	Allies	Enemies	NI	Total
War Coalition Participant Dyads ('t')	213	84	327	624
Non-Participant Dyads	262	172	2606	3040
	475	256	2933	3664

$x^2 = 376.9$
$df = 2$
prob. = .0001

Part B. 't+k' Comparisons: All Dyads

	't+k'		
	Allies	Enemies	NI
War Coalition Participant Dyads	34.1%	13.5%	52.4%
Non-Participant Dyads	8.1%	5.4%	86.5%
	Z=17.9 prob.=.0001	Z=7.2 prob.=.0001	Z=19.6 prob.=.0001

Part C. 't+k' Comparisons: Involved Dyads Only

	't+k'	
	Allies	Enemies
War Coalition Participant Dyads	72%	38%
Non-Participant Dyads	60.4%	39.6%
	Z=3.23 prob.=.0007	Z=3.23 prob.=.0007

Table 2 we have noted symbolically *how* War Coalition Participant dyads should differ from the others. These relationships are *specifically* tested in Tables 4 and 5. All but one of the eight possible relationships set out are confirmed. Let us turn now to Table 4 for a closer comparison of War Coalition Participant dyads and Belligerent dyads.

Part A of Table 4 demonstrates once more that the total pattern of 't+k' dyads derived from War Coalition Participant dyads is different from the pattern of 't+k' dyads derived from Belligerent dyads. Simply viewing the frequencies of dyad types reveals these differences. However, the chi-square statistic highlights the difference, indicating roughly that we could expect this configuration by chance only one time in a thousand. The null hypothesis is that the frequencies associated with War Coalition Participant dyads are not statistically different from those associated with Belligerent dyads. The chi-square is high enough to *reject* such a null hypothesis.

Part B addresses itself to the relationships set out under (b) in Table 2. Looking at *all* 't+k' dyads, War Coalition Participants produce a higher percentage of Allies at 't+k' and a lower percentage of Enemies than do Belligerent dyads (in terms of Table 2: L>Q and M>R). In part C of Table 4 we focus only on the "involved" dyads, those having future war interaction. However, the results are the same. War Coalition Participant dyads produce a higher percentage of Allies and a lower percentage of Enemies. In all four comparisons the Z-test was statistically significant at the .0001 level.[7]

Table 5 comparing War Coalition Participant dyads to Non-Participant dyads exhibits results very much the same as those in Table 4. The overall patterns, as shown in Part A are indeed quite different. In both Parts B and C, War Coalition Participant dyads produce higher percentages of 't+k' Allies (L>X). The only relationship to be disconfirmed is in Part B which looks at all dyads, where Non-Participant dyads produce a lower percentage of Enemies than War Coalition Participant dyads (Y<M, instead of M<Y). This is probably the result of the tremendously high percentage of NI dyads produced by Non-Participant dyads. This effect is controlled for in Part C where only the "involved" dyads are compared. Here the hypothesized relationship is confirmed (M is less than Y; the Z-test statistically significant at the .0005 level).

The comparison of War Coalition Participant dyads and Non-Participant dyads is a necessary one. This comparison indicates that the patterns produced by the War Coalition Participant dyads result from *more* than mere non-hostility. Non-Participant dyads also operationalize the non-belligerent experience, yet *do not* do as well as War Coalition Participant dyads in producing cooperative dyads at some future point—the 't+k' Allied dyads. Thus, the cooperative nature of war coalitions, as opposed to simple non-belligerency or non-involvement, may be seen as the influential factor in the future cooperation of War Coalition Participant dyads. In other words, while both War Coalition Participant dyads and Non-Partici-pant dyads lack a belligerency component in the relationship between the two nations in the dyad, the War Coalition Participant dyads have an extra, *positive* ingredient. These dyads have a positive cooperative aspect in the relationship between dyad members that Non-Participant dyads lack. The Non-Participant dyads were necessary in our analysis to draw a contrast between positive cooperation and mere non-involvement or non-interaction.

To sum up briefly, the working hypotheses presented earlier have been confirmed. War Coalition Participant dyads produce future patterns of war involvement that are statistically different from those of the other two groups. In addition, these differences are of the predicted type—more future allies and fewer future enemies for War Coalition Participant dyads.

A DIGRESSION: CHANCE

One brief digression is in order. So far we have compared War Coalition Participant dyads with the other two possible types of 't' dyads. There have been differences between the War Coalition Participant dyads and these other two groups. However, we must be sure as to the source of these differences. Although highly unlikely given the frequencies exhibited in Table 3, it is possible that all or most of the differences or variance is due to the patterns of the Belligerent dyads or Non-Participant dyads. That is, we now want to be sure that the differences discussed above are due (at least in large measure) to the patterns of the War Coalition Participant dyads and not dependent on the patterns of future behavior associated with the other two groups. This is really a question of which type of dyad provides us with the most information about future war behavior. If the Belligerent dyads or the Non-Participant dyads were to provide more information, explain most of the difference, we should be studying those dyads and not War Coalition Participant dyads.

One way in which to test for variance within the War Coalition Participant dyads or to test for the existence of distinct patterns is to set up a *null* hypothesis which predicts that War Coalition Participant dyads produce patterns no different from whose we could expect by sheer chance:

> Belonging to a war coalition makes no difference in terms of future patterns of dyadic war involvement—War Coalition Participant dyads will produce patterns that are not statistically different from those produced by chance.

This null hypothesis is tested in two separate ways in Parts A and B of Table 6. Looking at *all* 't+k' dyads, simple chance would predict that 33.3% of these dyads would be Allies, 33.3% would be Enemies, and that 33.3% would be NI (non-involved). In Part A we compare the actual 't+k'

TABLE 6
Comparing War Coalition Participant Dyads to Chance**

Part A. All Dyads

		't+k'			
		Allies	Enemies	NI	Total
't'	War Coalition Participant Dyads	34.1	13.5	53.4	100
	'Chance' (fair die)	33.3	33.3	33.3	100
		67.4	46.8	86.7	200

$x^2 = 13.9$
df = 2
prob. = < .01

Part B. Involved Dyads Only

		't+k'		
		Allies	Enemies	Total
't'	War Coalition Participation Dyads	72	28	100
	'Chance' (fair die)	50	50	100
		122	78	200

$x^2 = 10.2$
df = 1
prob. = <.01

Part C. All Dyads: 'Loaded Die'

		't+k'			
		Allies	Enemies	NI	Total
't'	War Coalition Participant Dyads	34.1	13.5	53.4	100
	'Chance' (loaded die)	15.6	8.5	75.9	100
		49.7	22.0	128.3	200

$x^2 = 12.3$
df = 2
prob. = <.01

** Cell entries are percentages.

dyads derived from War Coalition Participant dyads against such a chance distribution (observed against expected). As the chi-square test indicates, we *cannot* accept the null hypothesis that War Coalition Participant dyads produce patterns no different than those to be expected by chance. The patterns *are* different as indicated by the chi-square—a statistically significant difference.

In Part B, we drop the NI dyads, and deal only with those dyads which become involved in war again some time in the future, Allies and Enemies. In this case, pure chance would predict that 50% would be Allies and 50% Enemies. Again we can reject the null hypothesis that there is no difference, as War Coalition Participant dyads at 't' break down into 72% Allies and 28% Enemies at 't+k'. We may conclude then that war coalition participation leads to distinct patterns of future behavior, patterns that we could not expect from pure chance. As noted, *if* these patterns *were* no different from chance, the important differences in the earlier analyses would have derived from the Belligerent dyads and Non-Participant dyads. We now have a check on the "uniqueness" of the war coalition experience and the assertion that it is of interest to us, in the sense that it promotes future behavior not expected by chance and which is different from other possible experiences.

The analysis in Parts A and B of Table 6 make an important assumption, however. The assumption is that chance is playing with a "fair" die. In essence this means that in Part A chance was using a fair three-sided die, one that could fall as easily on one side as on any other; that, according to chance, over a long series of trials, Allies, Enemies, and NI's should even out. In Part B, we assume that chance is playing with a fair two-sided die (or a fair coin), which could just as easily come up Allies as Enemies. This, indeed, is what is meant by "chance."

However, one may argue that we should not be using such a fair die, that, in effect, history has loaded the dice and they are *not* fair. It is possible to argue that given international history it makes no sense to posit that a dyad is one third as likely to become Allies at 't+k', one third as likely to become Enemies, or one third as likely never to become involved again. If we look at the total dyads that exist at 't' (see Table 2, Part A), we see that War Coalition Participant dyads composed 15.6% of all 't' dyads (624/4006). Similarly, we note that 8.5% were enemies, those being the Belligerent dyads (342/4006), while 75.9% were non-involved at 't', the Non-Participant dyads (3040/4006).

We may use these time 't' distributions as one rough way to "load" the die. Given a survey of part of international history, we can posit that a dyad is three-quarters as likely to be non-involved and not one-third; or that a dyad is not one-third as likely to become Allies but only about one-seventh, and so on. Obviously, there are infinite ways in which to "load" the die. This is only one way, based on a convenient data set—the historical distribution of types of dyads at various 't' moments in history.

We may test the War Coalition Participant dyads against this "loaded" chance model, as we did above with two "fair" chance models. This is done in Part C of Table 6. Using a die loaded so as to more closely represent the probabilities of dyad types indicated by history, the War Coalition Participant dyads show even more clearly how disposed dyads composed of war coalition partners are to become partners again in the future. As in the rest of Table 6, the War Coalition Participant dyads demonstrate future patterns of behavior statistically different from those predicted by chance.

A brief summary of the above analysis in in order. This short digression with chance reinforces our notion that the war coalition experience produces future behavior patterns unique in terms of several types of comparisons. These patterns differ from those expected by chance and from those deriving from the other possible relationships that War Coalition Participants could have at 't'. The war coalition experience appears to dispose coalition partners away from becoming enemies at a future date, with only 13.5% of all War Coalition Participant dyads becoming Enemies (and only 28.3% of the involved War Coalition Participant dyads becoming Enemies). Thus, instead of asking what there is about war coalitions which produces Allies at some future date, the more crucial question is: what is there about those dyads which become Enemies which counteracts the non-belligerent influence of war coalitions? What works against the cooperative war coalition experience, against the "practice of operating together?" (Richardson, 1960: 197)[8]. In the next section we shall attempt to answer these questions. We will investigate some secondary variables to discover what characteristics are most representative of those War Coalition Participant dyads that become Enemies in comparison to those that become Allies, and also what variables might further reinforce the war coalition experience in encouraging future cooperation.

THE CHARACTERISTICS OF FUTURE ALLIES AND ENEMIES

VARIABLES AND HYPOTHESES

The first part of this paper was concerned with the question of whether or not there was a pattern of future war behavior associated with the war coalition experience. If so, then what was that pattern? How did it differ from comparable patterns of possible behavior? We answered these questions in the above analysis. In this section of the paper we are concerned with the "why" question. It appears that the phenomenon of war coalition cooperation itself is a powerful and adequate explanation of future cooperation in that the great majority of involved War Coalition Participant dyads again become war allies. Thus, the "why" focuses upon those war coalition partners that became future enemies; that percentage of dyads (13.5% or 28.3%) which may be conceived of as deviant cases. We want to look at an array of secondary variables in order to distinguish the dimensions of this deviant group, trying to discover on which characteristics they differ most from future allies, and in this way attempt to explain their deviancy. However, we must also investigate the characteristics of the 't+k' Allied dyads, for purposes of comparison and in order to delineate what secondary influences help promote future cooperation or conflict in addition to the simple fact of belonging to the same war coalition. Thus the remaining analysis will involve only those War Coalition Participant dyads that became Allies or Enemies at some 't+k': a sample of 297 dyads.

While the array of possible explanatory and discriminatory variables is vast, there do exist guidelines as to which may be the most promising factors to investigate. In the earlier study of war coalitions, several models were developed from major themes extant in the international relations literature (Starr, 1972: chap. 2 and 3). These models attempted to operationalize the realist and idealist views of international behavior through models based on power, major power status, military power, ties of ideology and community, and similarity of goals. A third major model was based on the character of each partner's participation in the war—the most useful model for the explanation of payoff distribution. Other models investigated the nature of the war, and the nature of the coalitions as they related to payoffs. Here, representative variables will be used to test the relationship of these models to the future nature of dyadic war experience. In addition, the distribution of payoffs and spoils (the dependent variable in the earlier study) will here be employed as an independent variable in explaining future war behavior. Several additional variables, noted below, will also be tested.

The power/realist models will be represented by a simple indicator. The dyad will be coded for whether it was composed of two major powers, two minor powers, or one major and one minor. The determination of major powers will follow that of Singer and Small (1972: 23-24). This indicator was employed as it provides the broadest cut across nation types in terms of "power" and, more importantly, in terms of styles of international behavior. This is particularly crucial given the nature of major power activity in international relations.

This indicator, as many of the indicators to follow, is set up in such a way as to use the differences between the two nations in the dyad as the explanatory factor. Many of the indicators are thus based on the notion of differences and discrepancies between the two nations in the dyad pair. The general proposition, therefore, is that following Wright's notions of distance and Rummel's formulations of field theory, the differences or distances between nations on specific attributes or behavior will affect their international behavior.[9] We will want to see if the dyad pair have had the same experiences (or attributes) and whether this makes any difference to future behavior.

Simply as a guide to research, as the first in a new set of working hypotheses, we may propose that similarity of great amounts of power will tend to make a dyad an Enemy in the Nextwar. Thus, Major Power/Major Power dyads should have a greater probability of becoming Enemies. This is based on a wide variety of statistical compilations indicating which nations have demonstrated themselves to be the most war prone. Data collected and analyzed by Wright (1965: chap. 9, append. 19, 20, 21), Richardson (1960: 173-176), and more recently by Singer and Small (1972: chap. 11) indicate that major powers, by whatever measure used, are the most war prone and account for a disproportionate amount of war in the international system. War may be considered a central activity of major powers, such that the interests and capabilities of major powers transcend the cooperative ties of the war coalition experience. In fact, George Modelski (1972) argues that war is a Great Power activity, and may be viewed as a disorder of the Great Power system. This may be seen as related to the general expediency effect that was discovered to influence the distribution of coalition payoffs (Starr, 1972: chap. 6). The effects of this major power indicator will be prominent in the following analysis.

The idealist model is represented by two indicators. In the earlier study an Ideology/Community Score was developed out of seventeen indicators (Starr, 1972: 44-46), many based on those used by Richardson. They were chosen to tap past and present cooperation and similarity along a variety of cultural, social, and political lines. Each nation was given an ideological/community score in terms of how it related to the war coalition as a whole. The first indicator to be used in the present study is the *difference* between the ideology/community scores of the two nations in the dyad (Ideology/Community Score Difference). In addition, we will also use the overall Coalition Ideology/Community Score, as a measure of the general idealist ties within the war coalition from which the dyad was drawn.

These two indicators attempt to tap feelings of community, "responsiveness," and "we-feeling." Russett (1963: 30; 1965: 25) has discussed responsiveness as the basis for community. Responsiveness may be seen as the readiness for compliance or favorable response which is necessary for sharing common values, interests, and non-violent conflict resolution mechanisms. Deutsch (1957) has looked for such things and found them necessary for a security-community, one in which the use of violence is not contemplated in the resolution of conflict. Pruitt and Snyder (1969: 178) have noted that:

> Similarity of race, culture, or ideology may to some extent restrain a state from the use of violence or reduce the level of violence employed. An empathetic mechanism is probably involved.

This is the basis of Deutsch's "security-community," and a major factor in the whole communications theory approach to integration.

We may therefore hypothesize that the larger the Coalition Ideology/ Community Score is (thus a greater degree of ideology/community in the parent coalition), the smaller the tendency for the dyad to become an Enemy in the next war. Similarly, the smaller the difference between participant Ideology/Community Scores, and thus the closer the two nations on the ideology/community scale, the smaller the tendency for them to become Enemies.

One sort of special experience within the scope of community relationships, is the presence or absence of a "last war." Although we have already posited a possible first order Markov-type process, it would be useful to isolate this special feature of past cooperation and community. The war coalition might have been an aberration in the history of the relationship between the dyad pair (or the "last" war might have been). Lastwar is defined exactly the same way as Nextwar, except we start at the *beginning* of the war coalition and scan *backwards* through history for the first time prior to the war coalition that the dyad pair was mutually involved in the same war. For the Lastwar, dyads were labelled Allies (t-k), and Enemies (t-k). Those dyads that never had a Lastwar were left blank. Simply, the war coalition always stands at some time 't'; the Nextwar is subsequent to the war coalition and stands at some time 't+k'; while the Lastwar occurs prior to the war coalition at some 't-k'. In both cases 'k' is some variable amount of years (which will be discussed further below). Of the 297 dyads which were involved in a Nextwar, 201 of them had also been involved in a Lastwar.

As a working hypothesis we may propose that having been involved as Enemies in a Lastwar then the higher the probability that dyads will be Enemies at 't+k', in the Nextwar. Again, this hypothesis assumes that the war coalition was but a temporary aberration with the Lastwar more accurately reflecting past traditions of conflict or cooperation of the dyad pair.

Similarly, we wish to isolate the effects of another long term influence on the past cooperation and conflict of the dyad pair, the ecological variable of a common border (Border). Richardson (1960: 176-183) was the first to point out empirically the importance of the effects of contiguity in the outbreak of war. He found that states have been involved in war in proportion to the number of their international frontiers, with a correlation coefficient of .77 for 33 nations. Weede (1970: 231), using DON data for 1955-1960, also concludes that "nations contiguous to many other nations are likely to participate in more violent conflict than geographically isolated states."

Contiguity, or the existence of a common border, may thus be seen as facilitating interaction of all kinds, including conflictual activities. This may be seen as deriving from Zipf's (1949) idea of interaction called the "principle of least effort." The · general notion of contiguity being associated with greater interaction has been tested by Cobb and Elder (1970: 26, 89), and supported in an analysis of a 49-nation world sample (with 1,176 dyads used as the units of analysis). Given the conclusions of Richardson, Weede, and others, we shall hypothesize that the existence of a common border between the dyad pair will be related to a greater tendency to become Enemies in the Nextwar.

Another indicator of war coalition community measures commonality of goals in a crude way (Goals). In the earlier study, each war coalition participant was coded for whether its pre-war and wartime goals were primarily status quo or redistributive. The present indicator tries to get at both types of goals held by the dyad members and the distance between them. Dyads were thus placed in one of three categories: one nation pursued status quo goals and one redistributive; both held status quo goals; or both held redistributive goals. We may propose two equally plausible working hypotheses:

(a) A dyad with a split in goals will be more likely to become an Enemy in the Nextwar;

(b) A dyad made up of two nations holding redistributive goals, and thus to some degree ambitious/expansionist/extrovert, will have a greater propensity towards becoming an Enemy dyad at a later point in history.

Continuing with the theme of past and present indicators of cooperation and the broader aspect of community, Pruitt and Snyder (1969: 178) have noted:

Cooperation between states can engender friendly feelings among the citizens that later act to inhibit the use of violence. . . The larger and more important the period of cooperation is, the more effective and durable such feelings are likely to be.

We could test this possibility, in part, by looking at two of the characteristics of war. The "larger and more important the period of cooperation" is operationalized by the length of war to the nearest half year,[10] and by the magnitude of deadliness associated with the war. This latter indicator (Deadliness) is based on Richardson's magnitude of a deadly quarrel: "The magnitude of a fatal quarrel is defined to be the logarithm to the base ten of the number of people who died because of that quarrel."[11] We may hypothesize that the longer and more deadly the war, the *less* the chance that the dyad will be an Enemy in the future.

Another indicator related to the war in which the coalition participated is called Typewar and is based on the general orientation of the side that won the war: again either status quo or redistributive. A third category termed status quo/offensive was devised for those winning sides that began the war with predominantly status quo designs and developed major redistributive positions by the end of the war. We may hypothesize that dyads from redistributive war, where the winners were after changes, expansion, spoils, and the losers were to lose heavily, will be more likely to become Enemies in future war.

Richardson, has, as noted earlier, suggested that the effects of war alignment cooperation decline over time. We have already confirmed his observation that war alliance has a pacifying effect on future behavior. To test the second part of his statement we have used two indicators of the same variable. One simply presents the number of years between the war coalition and the Nextwar (Timespan). The other sets up seven categories into which this length of time (Timecode) may be coded: under a year, 1-5 years, 6-10 years, 11-15 years, 16-20 years, 21-25 years, and over 25 years. Richardson fails to note when a future alliance might occur, but following his statements we may hypothesize that Enemy dyads will tend to occur when there is a greater temporal distance between t and t+k. That is, the longer the time between the war coalition and the Nextwar, the greater the probability the coalition will be an Enemy.

In addition to variables concerning the nature of the war, the war coalition fought, and its relationship to the Nextwar, we may look at two variables which describe the nature of the war coalition itself. The Coalition Ideology/Community Score discussed above may be counted as one of these indicators. The number of coalition partners is a second aspect we may deal with. Based on the findings dealing with expediency in the earlier study (Starr, 1972: 109-110), we may hypothesize that the larger the coalition, then the less general community within it, greater expediency influences, and thus a greater probability of future dyads being Enemies.

The third major model utilized in the earlier study was participation in the fighting of the war. A summary variable called Index of War Participation was devised which included whether a participant entered the war coalition at a crucial point in the war; whether this entry effected any pronounced change in the fortunes of the war in favor of the war coalition; whether or not the partner lost in a major military engagement during the war; and whether or not the participant engaged in at least one major victory against the opponent. The Index of War Participation summarizes the results of these four variables (Starr, 1972: 167-168). The indicator we will use here is the difference between the index scores of the dyad members (Participation Differences). The proposition here is that the greater the difference in wartime participation, the greater the likelihood that the dyad will be Enemies in the future. This is based on greater distance on the participation attribute moving nations away from each other.

Finally, several indicators based on the distribution of spoils were developed. We can look at both indicators of the type of payoff and indicators of differences or distances on the payoff/spoils scales. Burgess and Robinson (1969: 209) note that:

> The coalition that supplements collective benefits with private benefits is perceived as more effective, and the individual members of such coalitions perceive the other members of the coalition as more friendly, trustworthy, helpful, and cooperative.

In light of this we may hypothesize that dyads in which both members received spoils should be less likely to become Enemies in the future. For each of the two types of spoils—territory and indemnity—dyads were coded as to whether both received spoils or not, both received territory or not, both received indemnity or not. They were also coded for whether both failed to receive spoils or not, both failed to receive territory or not, both failed to receive indemnity or not. Finally, dyads were coded as to whether one received spoils while the other did not, one received territory while the other did not, one received indemnity while the other did not.

There were two other variables that indicate how much spoils were received, and can be used to look at the differences in spoils reception. For each coalition, for territory and indemnity, a simple mathematical average share was computed. For example, if there were four members to a coalition, then mathematically the average share would be 25%. If a partner had indeed received one quarter of the territory, his PAS (Participant Average Share) Territory would be 100%: having received exactly what his participant's average share of territory should be. If he received none of the coalition's territory then his score would be 0%; if he had received all of the territory in a four member coalition then his PAS Territory would be 400%—four times the amount of his average share. As you can see, the PAS score can range from 0%, for none of the coalition's territory or indemnity, through 100%, meaning a partner's exact mathematical average share of territory or indemnity, to an unlimited upward number (determined by the number of coalition partners) meaning he received X many times more of territory or indemnity than his average share should be. Both PAS Territory and PAS Indemnity were taken, and for the dyad we calculated the difference between the PAS score of each dyad member (Share of Territory Difference; Share of Indemnity Difference).

With the above variables we could test Arnold Wolfers' assertion (1962: 18) that any nation that "has been subjected to discrimination will, when its power permits, take some action to redress its grievances." We may hypothesize that the greater the difference between the PAS scores of dyad members, the more likely they will be Enemies in the Nextwar. Peripherally, this is related to Richardson's finding of revenge as a strong factor in the onset of war.

Because in the earlier study territory appeared to have a stronger impact than indemnity, another indicator based on the distribution of territory was developed. This consists of a simple question: in a dyad, was the PAS Territory of one member over 100% (thus more than expected), while the other was under 100% (less than expected)? It is hypothesized that such unfair distribution of the important spoil of territory would be a factor tending towards erosion of the cooperative experience. If the variable Unfairness of Territory Distribution is coded yes, it is suggested there is greater likelihood the dyad will become an Enemy dyad.

A final variable taps the overall differences in satisfaction with the results of the war. In the earlier study a variable called Degree of Fulfillment was developed to scale, albeit crudely, the degree to which prewar and wartime goals of each participant were fulfilled. Here we want to look at the difference between the Degree of Fulfillment score for the members of the dyad. Once more, we hypothesize that the greater this difference, the greater the likelihood that the dyad will become an Enemy dyad.

These variables and the set of working hypotheses are summarized for the reader's convenience in Tables 7 and 8. Table 7 presents each variable by name, a short description of what it indicates, and a note on the form the variable takes (dichotomous, nominal, interval). This last piece of information is useful in understanding which statistical tests will be used for each specific hypothesis (see Appendix II). Table 8 lists the twenty

TABLE 7
Variables Used in Study

Dependent Variable	
Name	**Description**
Nextwar	The type of 't+k' dyad derived from War Coalition Participant dyads: either Allies or Enemies (dichotomous)

Independent Variables	
Name	**Description**
Major Power/Minor	Describes dyad in terms of major power/minor power makeup; either major/major, minor/minor, or major/minor (trichotomous, nominal)
Ideology/Community Score Difference	An index was devised to measure each individual war coalition participant's ideology/community score; this variable indicates the difference between the two scores of the dyad members (interval)
Coalition Ideology/ Community Score	This variable is a war coalition summary score of all participants' ideology/community scores; it is used to show the community context of the coalition from which the dyad was drawn (interval)
Lastwar	This is the type of dyad the dyad members formed at some 't-k' past period in time; the <u>last</u> mutual war experience coded as either Allies or Enemies at 't-k' (dichotomous)
Border	This asks whether or not there is a common border between the dyad's members (dichotomous)
Goals	This looks at the combination of general goals held by dyad members while war coalition partners; either both redistributive, both status quo, or one redistributive and one status quo (trichotomous, nominal)
Length of War	This is the length of the war the war coalition fought to the nearest half year (interval)
Deadliness	This is the magnitude of deadliness of the war the war coalition participated in, expressed by Richardson's scheme of log to the base 10 of the number of people killed directly by the war (interval)
Timespan	This is the actual number of years between the end of the war the war coalition fought in and the beginning of the war the dyad members became mutually involved in (interval)
Timecode	Consists of seven coded categories for the number of years represented in Timespan (ordinal)
Coalition Size	Indicates the number of nations which were partners in the war coalition (interval)
Typewar	This labels the war the war coalition fought based on the general goals of the side that won: status quo, redistributive, status quo offensive (trichotomous, nominal)

TABLE 7 (Continued)

Participation Difference	This is the difference between war participation index scores of the two dyad members (interval)
BothSpoils	Asks whether both dyad members receive spoils, yes or no (dichotomous)
BothNotSpoils	Asks whether both dyad members fail to receive spoils , yes or no (dichotomous)
OneSpoils	Asks if one dyad member receives spoils while the other did not, yes or no (dichotomous)

These last three questions were also repeated as they apply to:

Territory	Indemnity
Both Territory	Both Indemnity
Both Not Territory	Both Not Indemnity
One Territory	One Indemnity

Share of Territory Difference	This is the difference between the PAS territory scores of the two dyad members, with PAS territory measuring the degree to which the dyad member received his mathematical average share of war coalition territorial spoils (interval)
Share of Indemnity Difference	The same as above, except for indemnity (interval)
Unfairness of Territory Distribution	This indicator codes whether or not one dyad member received more than his PAS share of territory while the other dyad member received less (dichotomous)
Goal Fulfillment Difference	This is the difference between the Degree of Fulfillment Scores of the two dyad members, with those scores scaling the degree to which each fulfilled pre-war and wartime goals (interval)

hypotheses in "if-then" form with the relevant variable in each hypothesis underlined. A code indicates which specific statistical tests were used, while another code indicates whether or not the hypothesis was confirmed. The next section will present the analytic basis for these judgments on confirmation. Each hypothesis will be tested beginning with simple bivariate relationships for the whole sample, then breaking the whole sample of 't+k' involved War Coalition Participant dyads into several analytic sub-samples. Finally, the analysis will move on to multivariate techniques.

HYPOTHESIS TESTING: DATA ANALYSIS AND METHODOLOGY

In this section we will deal with clusters of hypotheses as they relate to the models of international behavior noted above: power/expediency; ideology/community; the nature of war, the coalition, and participation;

TABLE 8
Working Hypotheses

Form: "If X then Y" (if X then the greater probability of Y occurring)

a) If <u>Major Power/Minor</u> consists of two major powers then Nextwar Enemies (++)(1.)

b) If smaller <u>Coalition Ideology/Community Score</u> then Nextwar Enemies (+)(2.)

c) If greater <u>Ideology/Community Score Difference</u> then Nextwar Enemies (+)(2.)

d) If <u>Lastwar</u> enemies then Nextwar Enemies (++) (1.)

e) If there is a common <u>Border</u> then Nextwar Enemies (++) (1.)

f) If <u>Goals</u> do not match then Nextwar Enemies (0) (1.)

g) If both hold redistributive <u>Goals</u> then Nextwar Enemies (0) (1.)

h) If <u>Length of War</u> is short then Nextwar Enemies (++) (2.)

i) If <u>Deadliness</u> is small then Nextwar Enemies (0) (2.)

j) If <u>Typewar</u> is redistributive then Nextwar Enemies (+) (1.)

k) If <u>Timespan</u> is greater then Nextwar Enemies (+) (2.)

l) If <u>Timecode</u> is coded higher then Nextwar Enemies (+) (1.)

m) If <u>Coalition Size</u> is greater then Nextwar Enemies (0) (2.)

n) If <u>Participation Differences</u> are greater then Nextwar Enemies (-) (2.)

o) If <u>OneSpoils</u>; <u>OneTerritory</u>; <u>OneIndemnity</u>; coded yes then Nextwar Enemies (-) (1.)

p) If <u>BothSpoils</u>; <u>BothTerritory</u>; <u>BothIndemnity</u>; coded yes then Nextwar not
    Enemies (-) (1.)

q) If <u>Share of Territory Difference</u> is greater then Nextwar Enemies (++) (2.)

r) If <u>Share of Indemnity Difference</u> is greater then Nextwar Enemies (-) (2.)

s) If <u>Unfairness of Territory Distribution</u> is coded yes then Nextwar Enemies (++) (1.)

t) If <u>Goal Fulfillment Difference</u> is greater then Nextwar Enemies (-) (2.)

KEY: ++ = hypothesis confirmed; + = weak confirmation; — = hypothesis not
confirmed; 0 = ambiguous; 1 = indicates the use of the chi-square statistic; 2 =
indicates the use of difference of means t-test and product moment correlation.

the temporal distance between the war coalition and the Nextwar; and the
influence of war coalition payoffs. The initial analysis will be bivariate,
searching for relationships between the variable under consideration and
the behavior of the dyad in the Nextwar. Several controlling variables will
then be introduced. In order to avoid the universal fallacy as discussed by
Alker (1965: 103), the total population of dyads will be subdivided in
several ways and the hypotheses re-tested for each of the resulting new
groups.

The first cut into the total sample will follow the example set by Singer
and Small in their studies of alliances (1966a; 1966b; 1968). In these

studies the time period, which is almost identical to the one under study here, was cut in two, using the year 1900 as the separation point. Singer and Small (1968: 255-256) argue that World War I and the years preceding it are qualitatively different from other wars and the periods preceding those wars. Following Singer and Small's example, this study will also use 1900 as a separation point.[1][2] The dyads will be separated into two groups: dyads which derive from war coalitions which were formed up to and including the year 1900, and dyads derived from war coalitions which were formed after the year 1900. These will simply be called nineteenth century Dyads and twentieth century Dyads.

A second cut at the total sample again tries to separate out the influence of the length of time that expired between conclusion of the war in which the war coalition participated and the occurrence of Nextwar. Thus we will attempt to control for this variable (as measured by Timecode) in the course of the bivariate analysis between Nextwar and the series of independent variables. Initially, two major groups are identified: dyads formed *less* than 25 years after the conclusion of the war coalition, and dyads formed *more* than 25 years after the war coalition (under 25 group and Over 25 group). This time split is based on studies such as those by Denton (1966), Denton and Phillips (1968), or Singer and Small (1972) which discuss cyclical patterns in international conflict. Possible explanations for such cycles include generational effects, sufficient time to forget the horrors of the last war, psychological and Freudian explanations, or the effects of a generalized arms race (Alcock, 1972). Nevertheless, 25 years emerges as the mean figure for the several cycles discovered.

Several more specific cuts will also be used for the Timecode control. The Under 25 group will also be subdivided into two groups: 0-5 years and 11-25 years. This will allow us to find any significant differences between the shortest period, 0-5 years, and the longest, Over 25. It also allows us a somewhat more detailed look at the larger Under 25 sample.

Finally, the total group will be cut in terms of the Major Power/Minor Power composition of the dyad. As has been noted above, the participation of major powers has been investigated and found to be a significant factor in the war propensities of nations. Singer and Small in their alliance studies have shown that major powers display patterns of behavior that differ from non-majors in regard to the relationships between war and alliance. As will be discussed in the analysis below, Major Power/Minor Power differences in large part stem from differences in the scope of activities of major powers as compared to other international actors. Major powers are disproportionately over-represented in terms of amount of international interactions (see McClelland and Hoggard, 1969), as well as in international war activity. Major powers interact with a greater variety of international actors in a greater variety of situations than do nations of lesser power status. Robin Jenkins proposes a "feudal" system model for international relations, based on the contention that:

> Interaction tends to be dependent on average power; there tends to be a lot of interaction between states that are powerful, less interaction between states that are powerful and others that are weak, and still less interaction between states that are weak. The amount of interaction seems strongly dependent on the *total power* of any pair of nations.[13] [Jenkins, 1971: 82].

Thus, the groups here will consist of dyads which are composed of two major powers (Both Majors) and all other dyads (Non-Majors). The Non-Majors group will be subdivided into dyads composed of two minor powers (Minor Powers) and Mixed dyads (one major and one minor). The analysis will concentrate on comparisons between Both Majors and Non-Majors and Both Majors and Minor Powers. As will be seen below, the effects of this controlling variable will be considerable, and will be expanded upon in the section dealing with multivariate analysis.

The bivariate analysis of hypotheses could be presented in a variety of ways, based on success of confirmation, type of methodology, and so forth. However, the analysis will be discussed in groups of hypotheses based on the substantive areas under which each was presented above. Each group represents in some way a conceptual view or model of factors that effect the ways in which nations acting in cooperation interact with one another. As can be seen in Tables 7 and 8, the hypotheses concern independent variables which differ in form. Thus as indicated in Table 8 and discussed in Appendix II, the hypotheses vary in regard to the statistical tests employed. These include difference of means t-tests, chi-square, and product moment correlations. Only those statistical values that are substantively relevant (and, in many cases statistically significant) will be reported in the text. The reader is reminded that Table 8 provides a convenient summation as to the degree of confirmation of each hypothesis.

Power/Expediency Hypotheses

Only one hypothesis will be discussed in this section. This will concern the makeup of the dyad in terms of major and minor powers. The general proposition is that dyads composed of two major powers will be more likely to become Enemies in the Nextwar. Taking the whole sample, this hypothesis is confirmed through the application of the chi-square test (X^2 = 9.98, p = .007). Dyads composed of two major powers (Both Majors dyads) are more likely to become Enemies than Allies, as 35.7% of major/major dyads become Enemies and only 19.7% become Allies. At the same time, dyads composed of two minor powers are less likely to become Enemies and more likely to become Allies (23.8% become Enemies while 38.0% become Allies). In this case we can reject the null hypothesis that Nextwar (the dependent variable which indicates whether a dyad at 't+k' is an Ally or an Enemy) is independent from Major Power/Minor (the independent variable which indicates the Major Power/Minor Power composition of the dyad).

We may now see how this relationship holds up when the total number of dyads is broken into several sub-samples. When the sample is divided by century, we find, interestingly, that there is no such relationship in the nineteenth century (x^2 = .82), so that the relationship between Nextwar and Major Power /Minor exists totally in the twentieth century (x^2 = 10.5, p = .005). In the twentieth century dyads that become Enemies are three times as likely to be Both Majors than are Allies (29.2% of Enemy dyads are Both Majors, while only 10.9% of Allied dyads are composed of two major powers). Thus the relationship is not a general one, but confined mostly to the present century. While, as noted, most war coalition partners remain partners in the future, and while World Wars I and II saw a general stability in alliance structure between them, the changes were most likely to have taken place in dyads composed by two major powers; that is, switches such as those of Italy and Japan from World War I to World War II, or China leaving the allied coalition in World War II, to become 't+k' Enemies with several of the major powers in the Korean War.

As is hinted at above, this hypothesis similarly is confirmed only for dyads which came into being Under 25 years from the end of the war coalition (x^2 = 14.69, p = .0006). Here Enemy dyads are more than twice as likely than Allied dyads to be Both Majors (43% to 20%). There are *no* Major/Major dyads in the Over 25 group. It appears that the high level of international activity that helps to identify major powers is such that it is difficult for major powers to interact over a long period of time without being involved in another war with former major power war partners. This is further evidence of the war-prone nature of major powers.

In general it does appear that dyads composed of major powers only are more likely to become Enemies in the future, particularly when compared to dyads composed only of minor powers. However, the hypothesis best fits those dyads formed in the twentieth century and which became engaged in war in less than 25 years. This hypothesis begins a cumulative argument concerning the important impact that the power status of dyad members has on future war involvement. This argument is augmented by further findings discussed below.

Ideology/Community Hypotheses

Six hypotheses may be grouped under this heading (b through g). Except for the last two which deal with the commonality of dyad members' goals, we find that hypotheses that predict a relationship between past associations, past indicators of responsiveness and community, do have an impact on future war behavior.

Two of these relevant hypotheses concern the overall index of ideology/community that might exist among and between war coalition partners. The first predicted that the smaller the overall Coalition Ideology/Community Score of the coalition the dyad came from, the greater the chance they would become Enemies. There is weak confirmation for this hypothesis. If one compares the average Coalition Ideology/Community Score for the Allied dyads to the average score for all the Enemy dyads one will find that the Enemy dyads do indeed exhibit Coalition Ideology/Community Scores whose average is statistically smaller than that of the Allied dyads (t = 3.45, df = 295, p = .0005). Correlating Coalition Ideology/Community Scores for all dyads to Nextwar, there is again weak confirmation (r = .17, p = .002). This means that higher scores tend somewhat to be associated with Allied dyads. While there is little explained variance, the relationship is in the right direction and statistically significant.

Similar general results are found in testing the other hypothesis based on the ideology/community index. This predicted that greater differences between the ideology/community scores of the two dyad members would be related to higher probabilities of being 't+k' Enemies. Again this is weakly confirmed, with the average difference in these scores for Allies statistically smaller than those of Enemies (t = 1.43, df = 295, p = .10). Again the correlation for the whole sample is weak, but in the right direction (r = −.09, p = .06). As a simple example, in the Second Balkan War, the Ideology/Community scores of Greece and Montenegro, Greece and Serbia, and Greece and Rumania were much closer to each other than those of Greece and Turkey. The first three pairs were in some way allied in the First World War, while the last formed an Enemy dyad.

The coalition ideology/community environment hypothesis holds about equally for both the nineteenth and twentieth centuries (r = .19 and .13 respectively), while dyad ideology/community differences seems to work only in the twentieth century and not in the nineteenth (r = −18, p = .009 in the twentieth century). The two hypotheses also have different impact in terms of time elapsed from the war coalition to Nextwar. The amount of coalition ideology/community relationship holds only for those dyads formed Under 25 years (r = .19, p = .002) and not for those Over 25 (r =

.08). A closer look reveals that all of the relationship is in the 11-25 Years group (r = .27) and not in the 0-5 Years group (r = .07). This indicates that the relationship is confirmed only for dyads in the middle range. At both extremes—0-5 Years and Over 25—the hypothesis fails. Immediate factors probably wash out ideology/community effects in the first five years, while time passed weakens the relationship for the Over 25 dyads. However, while the effects of a general ideology/community indicator seem to be middle term, the effects of differences in ideology scores seems to be short term. Hypothesis (c) seems to operate best in the more ideologically oriented twentieth century, in the short term when greater differences in ideology/community scores fail to inhibit, or act to incite war with a higher probability.

Turning to the major power-minor power composition of the dyad, we find a pattern which will emerge again and again in the testing of our hypotheses. In regard to coalition Ideology/Community for the Both Majors group there is *no* relationship (r = .09, p = .22), while there *is* for the Non-Majors (r = .14, p = .02). As seen from the Major Power/Minor hypothesis, the major power-minor power composition of the dyad effects the probability of whether a dyad becomes an Enemy dyad in a Nextwar. However, we will see that for almost every other variable, there rarely exists any relationship between that variable and Nextwar for dyads made up of two major powers, while there will exist a relationship for the others. This indicates that basically, a dyad made of two major powers is unaffected by other variables. The interests, war proneness, and character of major power dyads is the dominant variable and is thus not affected by other variables. This fits into the classic freedom-of-action, balance of power characterization of major powers, which features their ability to become involved in war with any nation whose interests conflict with their own in any particular circumstance. We can say that major/major dyads are more likely to become Enemies, but after that there is very little which we can say about major/major dyads, as very few variables have any effect on their behavior. For example, in this hypothesis, ideology/community scores for the coalition have no effect on future war allies and enemies for dyads made up of two major powers, while it did have a positive relationship for all other dyads. As another example, we find that there is no relationship between Ideology/Community Score Difference and Nextwar when using only the Both Majors group (r = −.076, p = .26), while there is a weak relationship for the Non-Majors group (r = −.10, p = .06) and a stronger one for Mixed dyads of one major and one minor (r = −.17, p = .03).

To summarize, these first two "idealist" hypotheses have been weakly confirmed. There is a tendency for those dyads which come from coalitions with lesser ties of ideology/community to become Enemies, and for those dyads where there is greater distance between the two members in terms of ideology/community to become Enemies.

Two other hypotheses concerned with interactions may also be considered confirmed. Both of these will appear in the multivariate analyses as important discriminators between 't+k' Allies and Enemies. The first of these concerns past interactions, and proposes that those dyads which were enemies in a Lastwar will be more likely to be Enemies in a Nextwar. This hypothesis is confirmed for the whole sample ($x^2 = 6.26$, p = .01). Enemies at 't−k' are twice as likely to be Enemies at 't+k' than they are to being Allies; ('t−k' Enemies makeup only 17.9% of 't+k' Allies while they constitute 35.7% of 't+k' Enemies). This means that in certain instances, we must study not only the previous experience (the war coalition experience) of two nations, but the war experience before that. French and German war coalition partnership in the Boxer Rebellion hostilities of 1900, for example, turns out be a far less reliable predictor of Nextwar activity (World War I) than the conflict which was labelled Lastwar for that dyad—the Franco-Prussian war.

For most dyads, however, this relationship is found in the twentieth century ($x^2 = 7.85$, p = .005), with no relationship in the nineteenth ($x^2 = .49$, p = .48). In the twentieth century, t−k Enemies make up 29.7% of t+k Enemies, but only 8.5% of t+k Allies. Similarly, the relationship between Lastwar occurs entirely among those dyads formed between 0-5 Years ($x^2 = 20.23$, p = .00001). For the 0-5 Year group, Enemies at t−k make up 52% of t+k Enemies, while making up only 7% of t+k Allies. There is absolutely no relationship between the two variables for Over 25 dyads or 11-25 Years dyads. Again it seems that the effects of a Lastwar are short term, (within 5 years) if felt at all. In addition, it will be most strongly felt by Minor Powers dyads ($x^2 = 6.5$, p = .01), where t−k Enemies make up 62.5% of t+k Enemies, while making up only 20% of t+k Allies. As before, there is no relationship between Lastwar and Nextwar for Both Majors dyads. So, for dyads formed in the twentieth century, by two minor powers (or at least not two major powers), within five years of the war coalition, the hypothesis is strongly confirmed. For the whole sample, it is still confirmed.

It was also hypothesized that the existence of a common border makes t+k Enemies more likely. Instead of a specific past interaction such as a Lastwar, this proposition infers that the opportunity to interact will make war more likely, worsened by the existence of possible territorial disputes. Again using a chi-square, this is confirmed for the whole sample of dyads, ($x^2 = 4.87$, p = .03). T+k Enemies are more likely to have a common border (30% do), than are Allies (only 17.4% do). There are no differences between the nineteenth and twentieth centuries, and no differences between the Over 25 and Under 25 groups. As a strongly ecological variable, systemic based and often bound to geography, Border is not affected by either historical time, or the Timecode between the war coalition and Nextwar: for all groups common border is related to a higher probability of the dyad being and Enemy dyad.

That is, until we come to the major power-minor power composition of the dyad. Dyads composed of two major powers show *no* relationship between Border and Nextwar (x^2 = .37, p = .54). However Minor Powers dyads again confirm the hypothesis, with Enemies twice as likely to have a common border than Allies (50% of Enemy dyads do, while only 23.5% of Allied dyads do; x^2 = 4.3, p = .04). The only group failing to display this relationship was Both Majors—those dyads composed of two major powers. Again, the characteristics of the major power dyad are overridden by the fact that the members are major powers. The interests of major powers being very broad, often global, transcend the effects of common borders. Minor powers, whose interests are more localized, find themselves more often in conflict with nations which are also minor powers, also with localized interests. The *lack* of a common border seems indeed to have a pacifying effect for Minor Powers dyads; a full 76% of Minor Powers dyads which became Allies, do *not* have common borders.

In terms of the broader study of war and its correlates and causes, these findings confirm earlier analyses by Richardson (1960) that contiguity may have the effect of promoting violent conflict. They also fit with the findings of Barringer (1972), who investigated the movement of conflicts into and out of violent modes of resolution. One of the major factors which tended to raise conflicts onto the level of violence was the existence of major power backing to minor power conflict. Such localized conflicts almost invariably involved minor powers with common borders.

Two final hypotheses concerned the broad range of goals held by dyad members. Hypothesis f suggested that if one member held status quo goals and the other member had redistributive goals, then the dyad would be more likely to be Enemies. Hypothesis g proposed that if both members held redistributive goals, the dyad would most likely become an Enemy dyad. The results of both are ambiguous. Neither can be confirmed for the sample as a whole, Allies and Enemies looking the same in regard to Goals.

Analysis by century is interesting as it provides two different patterns, accounting for the lack of patterns for the sample as a whole. In the nineteenth century, hypothesis (f) displays a very slim tendency towards confirmation, while (g) shows a tendency towards disconfirmation (x^2 =

3.44, p = .18). In the twentieth century the reverse holds: there is a tendency towards the confirmation of (g) and a tendency towards the disconfirmation of (f); (x^2 = 4.06, p = .13). Simply, this means that in the nineteenth century, dyads that became Enemies tended more to having goals which were split, but more so towards both having status quo goals; while in the twentieth century Enemies are more likely to both have redistributive goals.

Both hypotheses are disconfirmed, with no patterns emerging in any of the Timecode groups. As before, there are no patterns for the Both Majors group. The only group tested which demonstrates any decent relationships is the Minor Powers group. Here, (f) is disconfirmed and (g) is confirmed. For dyads composed of two minor powers, Enemies are more likely than Allies to have both dyad members with redistributive goals (45% to 27%). For minor powers, to whom certain expansive goals may be very important, and who especially do not want to lose in the pursuit of such goals to other minor powers, the clash of two expansive and possibly ambitious sets of goals produces a tendency towards future Enemy dyads.

In general, the results here follow those of the earlier study on the distribution of spoils. Ideology/community variables exhibit some tendency to predispose war coalition partners more favorably to one another. However this occurs within a general expediency framework, here operationalized by the failure to find relationships for the Both Majors sub-group. This holds true even for such prominent past interactions as a Lastwar, or the continuing influence upon interactions of a common border.

Hypotheses Concerning the Nature of the War, the Coalition, and Participation

This set of hypotheses deals with variables specific to the war coalition situation, looking at the length of the war, the deadliness associated with it, the type of war, the size of the war coalition involved, and differences in wartime participation by dyad members. Only the length of war and the type of war are confirmed as having significant relationships with future choice of Allies or Enemies.

It was proposed that the dimensions of cooperation would effect the amount of cooperation that was "learned" during the war coalition experience. Thus the shorter the war coalition experience—the shorter the war—then the greater the likelihood of dyad members to be Enemies. This hypothesis may be considered confirmed. The average length of the war for Allies is longer than that for Enemies (t = 2.36, df = 295, p = .01). Thus, in general, Enemies have participated in shorter wars than dyads which become Allies. For the whole sample we also obtain a weak but statistically significant correlation of .14 (p = .01). We may conclude the hypothesis is valid for the whole sample. While cooperation in war was a feature of the allied coalition in the Boxer Rebellion, a high percentage of Enemy dyads resulted. One element of this was the shortness of the period of cooperation.

While century has no effect (both the nineteenth century and the twentieth century groups produce similar correlations—.13 and .12 respectively), the hypothesis is confirmed again by Timecode. The results are most striking at the extremes: Over 25 produces a correlation of .27 (p = .04), and 0-5 Years a correlation of .16 (p = .03). There is no relation for the middle, 11-25 Year group. Nevertheless, the hypothesis displays its presence at the two ends of the Timecode scale. As before there is no relationship between Length of War and Nextwar for the Both Majors group (r = −.01, p = .46). This is as expected, the length of a war having no effect on the future behavior of major powers which have a great variety of interests, and a flexibility for conflict and cooperation that easily transcend the mere length of a war. For Minor Powers dyads, however, there is some confirming relationship (r = .21, p = .02). For minor powers who are more amenable to learning cooperation, who lack the far-flung and extensive interests of major powers, the length of the cooperative war experience is related to the future choice of allies and enemies, with longer wars related to future Allies, and shorter wars related to future Enemies.

In the same manner, it was proposed that the cooperative experience would carry more meaning the greater the sacrifice it involved. Thus it was proposed that the *less* deadly the war the more likely dyads would be Enemies. The hypothesis is disconfirmed for almost every group with two exceptions. For all Allies the average deadliness of their wars is not, as proposed, greater than the average deadliness for all Enemy dyads to a statistically significant degree (t = .69, df = 295, not significant). For the whole sample the correlation was similarly insignificant (r = .04, p = .25). By century, the twentieth century showed no relationship (r = .04), while the nineteenth century displayed the opposite relationship (r = −.16, p = .04). This indicates that for dyads formed in the nineteenth century, the greater the magnitude of the deadliness of the war, the more likely dyads were to be enemies. This might indicate hostile feelings developed during wars where there was a high cost for war coalition partners, and because the cost was high partners were prompted to expressions of revenge. This is only a possible, speculative reason for disconfirmation of the hypothesis. Turning to Timecode, the only group to confirm the hypothesis is the 0-5

Years group ($r = .13$, $p = .07$), and then only the slightest of tendencies. If the magnitude of death of a war has any effects at all, they are of the shortest run, and apply only to minor powers as the only other group to confirm the hypothesis, with the strongest relationship, is the Minor Powers group ($r = .215$, $p = .02$).

Along with the length of war hypothesis, the only other proposition to be at least weakly confirmed is the one dealing with the type of war.

This hypothesis proposed that dyads emerging from redistributive wars are more likely to be Enemies. For the whole sample the relationship is disconfirmed, having no relationship at all ($x^2 = .41$, $p = .81$). This may be because the nineteenth and twentieth centuries produce opposing relationships. The nineteenth shows some tendency to disconfirm the hypothesis, with Enemies more likely to from status quo wars rather than redistributive ones ($x^2 = 3.26$, $p = .19$). In the twentieth century group however, the opposite is found—Enemies indeed are more likely to emerge from redistributive wars than are Allies (25% to 11%); ($x^2 = 9.08$, $p = .01$). None of the four possible Timecode groups produces a chi-square pattern which is significant (the best being, $p = .34$). As usual, there were no patterns produced by the Both Majors group ($x^2 = .29$, $p = .86$). As with hypothesis (g) concerning dyad members holding redistributive goals, the Minor Power group did come through and support the hypothesis: for dyads composed of two minor powers, Enemies are more likely to come from redistributive war than Allies (55% to 25%; $x^2 = 7.15$, $p = .03$). Again, we may speculate that minor powers may see a greater stake in various types of expansive goals in terms of local or regional politics, and would be willing to go to war against other minor powers to obtain them.

The idea that redistributive war could break down bonds of cooperation was derived from the analysis of expediency in the earlier study. In that study also it was seen that larger coalitions tended to lack the more close-knit cooperation and ideology/community levels of smaller coalitions. Thus, we proposed here that the larger the coalition the more likely the dyad would be an Enemy. However, the results are ambiguous. For the whole sample there is no relationship between Coalition Size and Nextwar ($r = .08$). This is partially explained by opposite if weak patterns in the nineteenth and twentieth centuries. In the nineteenth century, larger coalitions display some tendency to be related to future Enemy dyads ($r = -.15$, $p = .05$), while in the twentieth larger coalitions tend to promote future Allies ($r = .11$, $p = .08$). It is possible that the weak differences between centuries reflect the more ideologically oriented inter-state relations of the twentieth century (for example, World War II, Korea, or even the Arab-Israeli wars), as opposed to the relatively more "expedient," less ideologically based relations of the nineteenth (as in the Second War of La Plata, the Crimea, or the Boxer Rebellion).

The size of the coalition appears also to reflect the nature of the time period between the war coalition and the Nextwar to be discussed below. There we will confirm the idea that cooperative effects decline over time. Here we can support that finding by noting that large coalitions are related to Allies if the dyads were formed within five years after the war coalition ($r = .195$, $p = .015$), while the larger the coalition the more likely the dyad would be an Enemy if the dyad was formed after 25 years ($r = -.21$, $p = .08$). Here the expediency effects of a larger coalition seem unable to emerge until after a sufficient time has passed to "forget" cooperation; until whatever cooperative effects of the coalition have dissipated.

Dyads composed of two major powers confirm the hypothesis, that larger coalitions lead to Enemies ($r = -.17$, $p = .075$). Simply following the fact that major/major dyads display a greater propensity to become Enemies in the future, the larger the coalition, with more chance that there will be major powers, the more likely they will become Enemies. This hypothesis, as noted, is based on the factor of expediency, which is indeed a hallmark of major powers. Minor powers dyads, on the other hand, are less expedient, more amenable to the effects of ideology/community as noted above, and less likely to let the expedient nature of larger coalitions overcome the cooperative nature of fighting in war as compatriots of other minor powers (especially in the short run in the more ideologically oriented twentieth century; $r = .35$, $p = .001$). In sum, while coalition size helps to support interpretation of other independent variables, it provides very little by itself.

The final hypothesis in this section deals with differences in participation in the war coalition. Since this was based on differences in effort and sacrifice—an area related to the discussion of Deadliness above—it should be no surprise that this hypothesis is not confirmed. The relationship proposed here is that greater differences in wartime participation would be related to greater tendencies to become Enemies. No matter how the sample is subdivided this relationship cannot be confirmed. For all Enemies the average difference in participation is not greater (and is in fact less than) the average difference in participation for Allies ($t = .39$). The correlation for the whole sample is non-existent ($r = .02$).

The only group to display even a tendency towards confirming the hypothesis is that group of dyads formed within five years of the war coalition: $r = -.11$, $p = 10$, (for the Over 25 group, $r = -.01$, $p = .47$). Inasmuch as the main explanatory thrust of the study on the distribution of payoffs within war coalitions is that of participation, we may ask what the present results mean. As noted in that earlier study, the investigation of payoffs was to be limited to the period immediately following the war coalition, a period of not more than five years. The present results indicate that the effects of the type of war participation do indeed have only immediate and short term consequences, with a slight tendency for greater disparities in war participation to be related to belligerency in the most immediate period after the war coalition. As a general explanatory factor in the future choice of Allies or Enemies, however, the war participation of the dyad members is of little or no use.

While hypotheses dealing with the specific war coalition situation provide us with some insight into the workings of other variables, and confirm other notions of expediency and time, the main contribution here is the relationship between Length of War and future war coalition partner behavior.

Temporal Distance Between
War Coalition Experience and Nextwar

In this section we will consider the hypotheses dealing with Timespan and Timecode. These propositions test Richardson's notion that the effects of alliance decline over time. We may generalize this idea to see whether the habits of cooperation developed in a war coalition situation are such as to decline over time. If this is the case then there would be a greater likelihood of Enemy dyads occurring the greater the temporal distance between the war coalition and the subsequent war experience. Both hypotheses provide weak confirmation for this relationship.

Simply, it is hypothesized that the greater the value of Timespan then the more likely it is for the dyad to be an Enemy dyad. While the average Timespan for all Enemies is indeed 13% longer than the average Timespan for all Allies, the difference is not statistically significant ($t = 1.01$, df $= 295$). Also for the whole sample, Timespan produces a correlation of only $-.055$ ($p = .17$) with Nextwar. Thus, for the sample as a whole (as well as for the nineteenth century and Both Majors dyads) the hypothesis cannot be confirmed. However there is weak confirmation in the twentieth century ($r = -.17$, $p = .01$) and stronger confirmation for dyads composed of two minor powers ($r = -.24$, $p = .008$). It seems that the war coalition experience leaves its effects on minor powers much more readily than on major powers, and then wears off in the manner proposed.

In a different, less powerful, but perhaps more appropriate manner, we can test the Richardson notion again by taking the Timespan between war coalition and Nextwar and breaking it into seven discrete categories. While not as precise as Timespan, Timecode does bunch dyads into rough categories, which may be a more useful way to generalize about them. In this form the data support the hypothesized relationship for the whole sample (x^2 = 17.59, df = 6, p = .007). More Enemy dyads form in the period after 21 years than do Allied dyads (46% of Enemy dyads form in this category as against 33.3% of the Allied dyads). At the same time, more Allied dyads form within the first five years subsequent to the war coalition than do Enemy dyads (44.1% to 27.7%).

While there are no significantly different patterns between Enemies and Allies for Timecode in the nineteenth century, it is *here* that Enemy dyads cluster in the over 21 year period, with 42% of the nineteenth century Enemy dyads forming after 21 years, and only 11% forming in the first five. However, as noted, this pattern is not significantly different from that of Allied dyads, (x^2 = 3.92, p = .69). There is a significantly different Enemy pattern in the twentieth century, but it *does not* confirm the hypothesis. In the twentieth century, Enemy dyads produce a double peaked pattern, being just as likely to form within five years as after 21 years (50% forming in the first five years following the war coalition, and 46% forming after 21 years). In terms of centuries, there are two different patterns, but neither seems to support the hypothesis.

The power of Richardson's observation, however, is demonstrated when we turn to the major power/minor power composition groups. There is a confirmation of the hypothesis for both both majors dyads and minor powers dyads. One confirmation, though, is weaker than the other. Both majors dyads which become Enemies are distributed as follows: 0-5 Years, 30%; 11-20 Years, 40%; 21+ Years, 30%, basically an even distribution, which does not really conform to the hypothesis. However, when compared to the major/major dyads that become Allies, the relationship is confirmed—more Allied dyads are formed within five years (36% to 30%), and less Allied dyads are formed after 21 years (21.4% to 30%).

The best relationship is once more found with dyads composed of two minor powers (x^2 = 26.20, p = .0002). Again there is the double peaked distribution, but again, compared to Allied dyads, Enemies are more likely to form after a longer period of time, and less likely to form within a short period of time following the war coalition. And, again, the independent variable shows greater explanatory strength with minor powers than major powers.

In sum, there does appear to be a forgetting of cooperation effect when comparing Enemy and Allied dyads. The two peaked distribution tends to indicate that if war coalition partners are not thrust against each other immediately after a war due, for example, to the distribution of payoffs (as in the Balkan wars, the wars of Mehmet Ali), then they will tend to take a long while to become Enemies. This analysis raises interesting questions about the relationship of time to the effects of international behavior, and suggests that time be used more explicitly in macro-quantitative studies over and above the simple use of short term time lags.

War Coalition Payoff Hypotheses

The final six hypotheses discussed deal with the impact that the distribution of war coalition payoffs has on the future selection of Allies and Enemies. These hypotheses go beyond the mere existence of a cooperative experience to ask if there must be some qualitatively positive aspect to the experience to make it one that will be remembered. Conversely, if war coalition members perceived themselves as being mistreated in the distribution of the rewards they felt were due to them, would this have a general impact on the future war behavior of these nations?

All of the hypotheses inquire if there was a difference between the two dyad members in their payoff experiences, and if this difference is related to their future war behavior. The hypotheses deal with spoils in general, a general fulfillment of war related goals, and with the specific types of war spoils, territory and indemnity. Of the six hypotheses, four are unconfirmed, and only two provide significant findings. Both these relate to differences in the distribution of territory. This would be consistent with the findings of the earlier study of war coalition payoffs where territory appeared to be a much more important aspect of international relations (Starr, 1972: chaps. 7 and 8).

Briefly, one set of hypotheses proposed that if only one member of the dyad were to receive spoils (either territory, indemnity, or both) while the other member did not, then the dyad would more likely be an Enemy. The same relationship is proposed specifically for territory and specifically for indemnity. All relationships tested, except for one group, disconfirm the proposed relationship.[14] In contrast, another group of hypotheses propose that if both members of a dyad receive spoils, or both receive specifically territory, or both receive indemnity, then it is *less* likely that the dyad will be an Enemy. The results here are highly ambiguous. For the whole sample, the relationship is reversed—Enemies are *more* likely than Allies to have both members of the dyad receive some sort of spoils (65.5% to 51.2%; $x^2 = 4.42$, p = .035). The same relationship is true for territory ($x^2 = 3.39$, p = .065) with Enemies more likely than Allies to have both dyad members receive territory (36.9% to 25.4%). Only for indemnity is there no relationship at all ($x^2 = .024$, p = .87), also disconfirming the hypothesis.

For the nineteenth century, there are no relationships exhibited between the three spoils variables and Nextwar. The relationships found for the whole sample, the association of both dyad partners receiving spoils and specifically territorial spoils with future Enemies, is based only on patterns produced in the twentieth century. Thus, the proposition that dyad members are more likely to become future enemies if they both receive spoils from a common war coalition, is valid only for the twentieth century, (BothSpoils: x^2 = 4.26, p = .039; Both Terr: x^2 = 7.196, p = .007). For the sample as a whole there was no relationship between BothIndemnity and Nextwar. For the nineteenth century there was also no relationship. This concurs with findings in the earlier study that indemnity seems to be of much less importance than territory to coalition partners.

In the twentieth century the hypothesis is confirmed with indemnity. In the twentieth century, having both dyad members receive indemnity was indeed a pacifying influence. Enemies were less likely to have both receive indemnity than Allies 3.7% to 24.8% (x^2 = 4.68, p = .03). Following arguments developed in the earlier study, it seems that indemnity *can* be used to demonstrate coalition good will and cooperation. Indemnity is the type of spoils, because of its unimportance, that can be distributed to partners for cooperative symbolic purposes, as side-payments of the type discussed by Burgess and Robinson (1969: 194-218).

It again appears that the effects of a variable—here the distribution of spoils—is not a long term one. For the Over 25 group there are no relationships between the three spoils variables and Nextwar. For the shortest range group, 0-5 Years, the patterns produced in the twentieth century recur: for territory in particular, Enemies are more likely to be dyads where both dyad members receive territory (44.8% to 22.4%, x^2 = 4.55, p = .03). Also, the hypothesis holds for indemnity; the cooperative effects of indemnity are manifested as a very short run phenomenon. Allies are more likely to have both receive indemnity 35.2% to 8.0% for Enemies (x^2 = .02). For spoils in general, however, there is no relationship for dyads formed within five years (BothSpoils, x^2 = .87, p = .35). Thus again, the hypothesis is disconfirmed for two of the three spoils variables used to test the hypotheses.

We begin a very important thread in our analysis by noting that there are no relationships produced in chi-square tests between the spoils variables and Nextwar for the group composed of two major powers. For Both Majors dyads we have another indication that spoils have little effect. For major powers, even territory seems to have no effect on future war behavior. For minor powers, however, spoils are important. For the Minor Powers group, the hypothesis is disconfirmed for Both Spoils with another reversed relationship: more dyads composed of two minor powers that become Enemies are more likely to have both receive spoils than those becoming Allies (70.0% to 43.2%; $x^2 = 3.59$, p = .06). This is based mostly on the territorial aspect, as the same reversed relationship holds for territory, (70.0% to 24.7%; $x^2 = 12.78$, p = .0004). Territory appears to hold an important place for minor powers. Fitting nicely in with the results for goals, and type of war based on goals, minor powers value territory, which tends to generate more conflict when both receive territory. The Balkan wars preceding World War I are classic examples. *How* the territory is distributed in terms of the dyad members is then the key question, and the discussion below provides some interesting and important answers.

Both of the strongly confirmed hypotheses deal with the *how* of territorial distribution. Recall that for each coalition which received territory a score was produced for each coalition partner indicating whether that partner received more, less, or the same amount as the partner would have received had the territory been distributed strictly according to the number of partners in that coalition. One hypothesis predicted that the larger the difference between these scores for the two dyad members, then the more likely the dyad will be an Enemy. Given the indications that territory does seem to make a difference for a variety of groups and the sample as a whole, it is not surprising to note that the hypothesis is confirmed.

For all Allies the average difference in territory share is smaller, and significantly so, than the average for all Enemies (t = 2.98, df = 204, p = .005). Again, for the whole sample, Share of Territory Difference correlates $-.24$ with Nextwar (p = .001). Both these statistics indicate that the hypothesis is confirmed for the sample as a whole. There is *no* difference here, in terms of centuries, the relationship is not affected by historical time period (nineteenth century: r = $-.37$, p = .004; twentieth century: r = $-.22$, p = .004). Similarly, no matter how one cuts the Timecode groups, the hypothesis is confirmed, indicating that the length of time from war coalition to Nextwar also does not affect the impact of territorial differentiation between dyad partners (Over 25: r = $-.43$, p = .008; Under 25: r = $-.22$, p = .002; 0-5 years: r = $-.32$, p = .001).

The only group that fails to confirm this hypothesis is that composed of two major powers (r = 0.05, p = .40). For all other, Non-Majors dyads the relationship still holds (r = $-.27$, p = .001). The disparity between scores which indicates the amount of territory received against a neutral mathematical expectation produces the predicted relationship for the whole sample, for both periods of historical time, and for the different periods measuring the passage of time. However, it does not hold for Both Majors dyads. Again, territory[15] demonstrates a pervasive importance, but not in the future behavior of major powers, who, in dealing *with one another* appear to be only minimally affected by past war coalition characteristics or events, and are much more attuned to factors expedient and situational.

A related hypothesis is also confirmed. It simply proposed that if a dyad consisted of one member which received more territory than mathematical equity would predict, and a second member which received less than that which mathematical equity would predict, then that dyad would more likely be an Enemy. For the whole sample, Enemy dyads indeed were more likely to demonstrate this split in Unfairness of Territory Distribution than Allied dyads: 63.2% of Enemy dyads were so split, while only 45.2% of Allied dyads were ($x^2 = 4.365$, p = .04).

This hypothesis was confirmed for all Timecode groups, again indicating that the relationship is not affected by the passage of time, (0-5 Years: $x^2 = 4.59$, p = .03; Over 25: $x^2 = 3.60$, p = .06). In fact, for the Over 25 group, *every* Enemy dyad possessed this characteristic (compared to 54.5% for Allied dyads). The hypothesis was also strongly confirmed for all Non-Majors dyad, it being no surprise that Both Majors dyads showed no relationship at all; (Both Majors: $x^2 = .051$, p = .82; non-Majors: $x^2 = 6.71$, p = .009).

One compelling point to note is that of the Enemy dyads in which this split occurred, 53% became Enemies in the 0-5 year period ($x^2 = 15.2$, p = .009). This is in contrast to the fact that a large percentage of Enemies tend to become Enemies after a relatively longer passage of time. The importance of territory, and the effect of the disparity of its distribution is confirmed. For dyads not composed of two major powers having both receive territory produces a tendency towards becoming Enemies. We see now that much of this tendency is related to the conflictual nature of an *unequal* distribution of territory—a confirmation of the basic notion behind the testing of spoils variables discussed earlier. For territory, valued more by minor powers, (or seemingly valued more), the disparity in reception from a parity norm based on a simple numbers of partners appears to create future hostilities (or is an indicator of conflict at the time the war coalition distributed payoffs). This would be especially true if the dyad were made up of two minor powers, with the member receiving less territory wondering why a nation of the same status should receive more of something that might help raise that status. These relationships and effects were not noted for indemnity, nor for general satisfaction of goals as tested in the relationship between Goal Fulfillment Difference and Nextwar.[16]

One note, however. While this hypothesis was confirmed in the nineteenth century (x^2 = 4.86, p = .03), it was not in the twentieth (x^2 = .97, p = .32). This may be due to the emergence of other factors in the twentieth century such as ideology, the nature of the settlements of the two World Wars which make up most of the twentieth century dyads, or it might also indicate a changing attitude towards territory.

As was noted in the earlier study, albeit in the form of specific references to wars such as Bismarck's various wars of German unification, the Balkan wars, and the wars of Mehmet Ali, we can say that there are important consequences stemming from the manner in which the fruits of war are taken and distributed. Territory especially seems to have an effect on future war behavior of coalition partners. Cooperation, which may decline over time, may also decline if certain territorial stakes are involved.

HYPOTHESIS TESTING: SUMMARY

We have now an idea of which hypotheses concerning future outcomes for war coalition partner dyads have some explanatory value and which have not. Six variables would seem to be of *little* value: Participation Differences, OneSpoils, OneTerritory, OneIndemnity, Share of Indemnity Difference, and Goal Fulfillment Difference. Other hypotheses span a continuum of confirmation. The most salient variables in relationship to Nextwar are: Major Power/Minor, Lastwar, Border, both members receiving territory, and differences in territory received. The other variables all produce some degree of confirmation for their relationship with Nextwar.

The reader must note, however, that the statistical relationships in even the best cases are fairly weak. The most compelling result we have produced so far—the strongest influence—is that of simply being a war coalition partner. That fact is related to an overwhelmingly non-belligerent set of future relationships with one's war coalition partners. After that we find a variety of *tendencies*, albeit weak ones, which explain to some degree why 28.3% of the War Coalition Participant dyads that do become involved in future war become involved as Enemies. (Or, why 13.5% of all War Coalition Participant dyads "go bad," and become Enemies in the future.) Separately, few of the variables tested have shown extraordinary explanatory power. Skjelsbaek (1971: 59) has provided us with some pertinent remarks on how to interpret such results. Concerning the

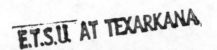

relationship of intergovernmental organizations (IGOs) to war (also studied at the dyadic level) he notes:

> The probability of a pair of nations becoming involved in war may be compared to the probability of persons getting lung cancer. In *absolute* terms both probabilities are very low. However, if a person smokes cigarettes, and a pair of nations substantially reduces its number of shared IGO memberships, the probabilities of getting lung cancer and fighting on opposite sides in a war, respectively, are *relatively* much higher than they would otherwise have been.

Instead of comparing the probabilities of lung cancer and war, we may substitute the probabilities of two war coalition partners becoming enemies at some time subsequent to the war coalition. We have seen that this is a "rare" occurrence. As Skjelsbaek notes, this outcome will be made somewhat more probable, within a limited range of occurence, by the existence of certain factors. Here, these factors seem to be dyads composed of two major powers, the existence of a common border, a Lastwar experience, and differences in the distribution of territorial spoils. What we wish to know now, is how these variables interact, and what effects they might have in combination. That task will be carried out in the following section describing the use of discriminant function analysis.

First, several further observations must be made concerning the results of the hypothesis testing analysis. In addition to highlighting the acceptance, rejection, and relative worth of each hypothesis, several other points have been brought to our attention. Some of the variables produce effects that are timebound in that they occur only in one of the two century-based groups, or produce opposite patterns in the two centuries. Some important examples of the former behavior are major power-minor power composition and Lastwar, which, as other variables, produce relationships only in the twentieth century. This was more often the case than the reverse. The number of coalition partners and Goals are examples of the latter point, where opposite relationships are produced. The use of historical time groups has allowed us to test the generality of the hypotheses in terms of historical era, to see which variables were operative in the past, and which have been operative in more recent times.

Secondly, we have seen that most of the variables under consideration have what would be considered short term effects.[17] The most consistent result of the analysis by groups of dyads based on the number of years between the war coalition and the Nextwar was the failure to find relationships with the Over 25 group. The dyads falling in this group appear much less affected by the variables tested, and thus support the notion that after a certain length of time the previous experience (the war coalition) becomes less and less relevant to the international war behavior of former coalition partners. There are some variables which are constant—the ecological nature of Border is the prime example of a variable whose effects are present even after 25 years. Similarly, the size of the coalition, and differences in territory distribution are valid even after 25 years. Thus, while several relationships may be presented in general terms, most of the results are meaningful only in the relative short term, for a period generally less than 25 years after the war coalition experience.

Finally, the very striking difference in groups based on different Major Power-Minor Power composition was revealed. Simply, dyads composed of two major powers were more likely to become Enemies in the future. Of the total 624 War Coalition Participant dyads, 84 were composed of two major powers. Of these Major/Major dyads, a full 36% became Enemies at t+k. There were 307 dyads composed of two minor powers, yet of these only 20 or 6.5% became Enemies at t+k (using a Z-test, Z = 7.10, p = .0001). Above analyses clearly indicate that major/major dyads are more likely than other dyads to become Enemies. However, after this there is very little that can be said for major/major dyads. They differ from minor/minor dyads across almost every hypothesis, and do so by producing no relationships with most of the variables. Once a dyad has been identified as composed of two major powers, its basic characteristic has been set forth: the dyad has a higher probability of being an Enemy and will tend to be unaffected by other influences. Minor power dyads on the other hand, are affected by almost all of the other variables and in the predicted directions. Minor powers are subjected to the influences of ideology/community, of coalition characteristics, of spoils distribution, and so on, while major powers are not. The fact of being a major power, with broad areas of interest both geographical and functional, with strong expediency-oriented behavior, must remain as flexible as possible. Perhaps a requisite of being a major power is war proneness, as Wright, Richardson, and Singer and Small have pointed out (see also Jencks, 1973). If so, a pair of major powers is most likely to be war prone. The balance of power-like flexibility exhibited and needed by majors overrides the influences hypothesized and studied here. Dyads composed of two major powers have belligerency built in, and thus show few, if any, relationships to other variables supposedly related to future belligerency. The differences between Both Majors dyads and Minor Powers dyads will be reinforced in the following multivariate analysis section.

MULTIVARIATE METHODOLOGY: DISCRIMINANT FUNCTION ANALYSIS

The bivariate analysis has provided us with a preliminary indication of which variables are associated with war coalition dyads that become Enemies in the Nextwar. The next step, however, is to use multivariate techniques for a clearer, yet more complex view of international relations, a very complex subject.

For this study multivariate techniques were used which permitted the analysis of a dichotomous dependent variable: was the dyad an Ally or Enemy in the next war?[18] Discriminant function analysis is a technique which will do this, permitting "an evaluation of the relative power of a number of predictor variables to discriminate between two or more a priori groups" (Kornberg and Frasure, 1971: 699). Here, the two a priori groups are the two involved 't+k' groups: Allies or Enemies. Allan Kornberg and Robert Frasure summarize the utility of discriminant function analysis (1971: 699):

> Very briefly stated . . . . the technique allows for the combination of multiple variables into a linear function that will best discriminate between two (or more) a priori groups. That is, the variable that shows the greatest difference between groups is considered first. Then, given its ability to discriminate the groups and intercorrelation with all other items, the next most important variable is evaluated with respect to its additional contribution. The process continues through all the variables.[19]

This is indeed exactly what we wish to accomplish—to find which characteristics of dyads that become Enemies best set them apart from those which once again become Allies.

From the bivariate analysis 19 variables were selected to be used in the stepwise discriminant function analysis. These are listed in Table 9, along with four additional variables. From the earlier study two variables have been included based on the Gini Index of inequality. GINI Territory and GINI Indemnity indicate how equitably the spoils were distributed across the whole coalition. BothFail to Get Spoils and BothFail to Get Territory are related to BothSpoils and BothTerritory. They simply ask if both members of the dyad *failed* to receive spoils. Of the 23 variables used, 21 were entered into the analysis. Unfairness of Territory Distribution and OneSpoils were excluded from the analysis by failing to meet the minimal entry criteria of the computer program. The 21 variables entered produced an F of 3.31 (df = 22, 274; p = .001). This statistic reflects the aggregate power of the function for discriminating between groups.

In addition, the program produces at each step a matrix indicating the number of cases, here dyads, classified into each group based upon the

TABLE 9
Variables Entered into the Stepwise Discriminant Function Analysis
In Order of Entry

Variable Entered	F At Entry	Stepwise Multiple F	% Correctly Grouped
1. Major Power/Minor	9.85	9.85	49.0
2. Border	8.22	9.15	63.3
3. Share of Territory Difference	8.99	9.27	62.0
4. Lastwar	9.00	9.39	67.0
5. GINI Indemnity	4.97	8.61	69.0
6. Coalition Ideology/Community Score	13.04	9.65	68.0
7. Ideology/Community Score Difference			
8. Lenth of War			
9. BothIndemnity			
10. Deadliness			
11. Goal Fulfillment Difference			
12. GINI Territory			
13. Goals			
14. Participation Differences			
15. BothTerritory			
16. BothSpoils			
17. BothNotTerritory			
18. Typewar			
19. Coalition Size			
20. Timespan			
21. BothNotSpoils			
	.027	3.31	73.0

variables entered. After the twenty-first variable this matrix was:

	Allies	Enemies
Allies	154*	59
Enemies	21	63*

The starred entries represent the number of cases "correctly" identified—discriminated—on the basis of the variables entered. Here, 72% of the Allied dyads and 75% of Enemy dyads were correctly identified, for a total percentage of correctly grouped cases of 73%.

Looking back to table 9 the reader will notice that the "F at Entry," "Stepwise Multiple F," and "% Correctly Grouped" were included only for the first six entered variables, and the last variable. The final result was included to give an overall picture of the discriminating power of all the variables that met the miniman entry criteria in the program. However, only the first six variables produced an "F at Entry" significant at least at the .05 level. These are the variables on which we will now concentrate.

Note that the multivariate technique has highlighted the *same* variables called to our attention by the bivariate procedures. The Major Power/Minor Power distinction retains its prominent place as the first variable entered. The portrait of an Enemy dyad developed through bivariate analysis—a dyad composed of two major powers, with a common border and with a belligerent war experience preceeding the war coalition—is reinforced here. Major Power/Minor is entered first, Border second, and Lastwar fourth. In the third position is Share of Territory Difference, reinforcing the observations made earlier on the role of territory in identifying future enemy dyads.[20] These four variables correctly group over two-thirds of the dyads. That is, on the basis of these four variables only, the future Nextwar status of more than two-thirds of the dyads can be correctly predicted.

There are three dyads which became enemies at 't+k' which combine these variables: are composed of two major powers, have a common border, and fought against each other in a Lastwar. That is, there are only three dyads that show all three of these traits together, but they create a small set of classic international enemies:

Dyad	War Coalition	't+k' War as Enemies
Austria-Italy	Boxer	World War I
France-Germany	Boxer	World War I
Japan-Russia	World War I	Russian Intervention

It is interesting that only after these very "realist" variables are entered as to their ability to discriminate between dyads that "idealist" variables are entered: Coalition Ideology/Community Score entered sixth, and Participation Differences entered seventh. It is also useful to note those variables that were not entered, or entered last, thus indicating much weaker discriminatory power. The two variables not entered concern differences in spoils experiences. Their explanatory power is accounted for by Share of Territory Difference, the third variable entered (see note 20). Variables whose F scores never rose above one, and are entered after the first six are: Goal Fulfillment Difference, Goals, Participation Difference, Type of War, Timespan, and Deadliness. Number in coalition does begin with an F value of 2.05, but drops to .36 after the first two variables are entered.

The analysis reported immediately above quite nicely separates those variables which are important (in discriminating Enemy dyads from Ally dyads) from those variables which are unimportant in this regard. By multivariate analysis we have checked for the interaction of variables, and have come up with results similar to the earlier bivariate analysis. The overwhelming non-belligerent effect of common war coalition experience is more likely to be broken by dyads with a common border; by dyads whose members have a large difference in the share of territory received; by dyads who were enemies in a Lastwar; by dyads from coalition with lower Coalition Ideology/Community Scores.[21]

The premier factor in terms of discriminating power is Major Power/Minor. Dyads composed of two major powers are more likely to become Enemies and the discriminant function analysis indicates this fact even taking into account all the other variables. We have seen previously that the bivariate analysis was unable to help us understand which major/major dyads tended to be Enemies and which Allies beyond the general statement that major/major dyads have a higher probability of becoming Enemies. In order to probe further into the nature of major/major dyads a separate discriminant function analysis was performed on the Both Majors group. Only three variables were entered so that their F-value at entry was at least at the .05 level of probability. The first variable entered, and therefore the best discriminator of Allies and Enemies *within* the Both Majors group is OneSpoils, which still only correctly groups 7 of the 30 Enemy dyads. The other two variables are Lastwar and Coalition Size. Together, however, these three variables correctly group 65.2% of the Both Major dyads.[22] This indicates that for dyads composed of two major powers, one might still be able to predict close to two-thirds of the cases by three variables: if the dyad had one member receiving spoils while the other didn't; if there was a Lastwar in which the dyad members were Enemies; and knowledge of the size of the war coalition. Larger coalitions tend to produce Enemies, even for major/major dyads.

Just for contrast, a discriminant function analysis was run for Minor Power dyads. The contrast between the variables entered for the Both

TABLE 10
Discriminant Function Analysis:
Both Majors Group and Minor Powers Group

Variable Entered (only those with significant F values)	F at Entry	Stepwise Multiple F	% Correctly Grouped
a) Both Majors Group			
OneSpoils	3.94	3.94	63.8%
Lastwar	3.67	3.88	63.8%
Coalition Size	5.18	4.47	65.2%
b) Minor Powers Group			
BothTerritory	16.92	16.92	74.2%
Unfairness of Territory Distribution	7.92	13.02	70.3%
Timespan	6.38	11.28	80.2%
Share of Territory Difference	9.93	11.72	84.1%
GINI Indemnity	3.35	10.28	83.1%
Goals	4.18	9.55	84.1%
Border	3.02	8.79	83.1%
Deadliness	1.97	8.02	85.1%
Goal Fulfillment Difference	2.09	7.44	86.1%

Majors and Minor Powers group is striking. First, *nine* variables were entered for the Minor Powers with significant F values, (see Table 10). These nine variables correctly grouped 86% of the minor/minor dyads into Allies and Enemies. The variables stressed the spoils and payoff aspects of the war coalition, as well as common Border, Goals, deadlines of the war, and Timespan; all reinforcing the relationships that emerged from bivariate hypothesis testing. We can see how different the two groups are, with *no overlap* from the three significant variables entered for major/major dyads to the nine variables so entered for minor/minor dyads.

In summary we can say that the discriminant function analysis has shown that the variables selected can be used to predict or group a large proportion of our cases correctly into Allies and Enemies.

CONCLUSIONS

In the opening pages of this paper two sets of questions were explicitly addressed. Because very little systematic research had been done on what effects common participation in war might have on future war behavior, we first wished to know if war coalition partnership had an impact on the choice of future allies and enemies. One way to test this question was to establish the "uniqueness" of the patterns of the future behavior of war coalition participants—by dyadic analysis—and then to see if the patterns were as hypothesized. It was proposed that the war coalition experience should be related to high frequencies of cooperative behavior in future wars and lower frequencies of belligerency. The data presented provided evidence supporting the "uniqueness" of the war coalition experience by contrasting the consequences of that experience with the consequences of the two other possible experiences war coalition partner could have had. As hypothesized, the consequences of war partnership appear to be more future partnership; the consequences of belligerency appear to be more future belligerency; and the consequences of non-participation appear to be more future non-participation.

In the quest for those factors regarded as "causes and correlates" of war we have delineated and investigated one such correlate. We have shown that the war coalition experience has a distinctive effect on the future choice of Allies and Enemies. The question was then posed—what is there about wartime cooperation that creates this effect? What factors are related to the future patterns of war behavior of war coalition participants? Inasmuch as the tendency towards future non-belligerency for the War Coalition Participant dyads was fairly strong and clear, this question was revised: what are the characteristics of future Enemy dyads that subordinated the cooperative, non-belligerent effects of war coalition participation?

To begin the task of finding some answers to the above questions, 20 working hypotheses were developed (see Table 8), 12 of which provide clear, if weak, tendencies which explain portions of the variance related to becoming Allies or Enemies. Using discriminant function analysis to deal with the multivariate framework created from bivariate analysis, the variables that best descriminated between Allies and Enemies were the major power-minor power composition of the dyad, whether or not there was a common border, the equity in the distribution of spoils, and whether or not the dyad members had been allies or enemies in a war previous to the war coalition. Finally, differences in ideology/community were also useful in discriminating between Allies and Enemies, indicators of this variable being entered sixth and seventh.

If we look at three of the four best discriminatory variables—Major Power/Minor, Border, Lastwar—we may be understandably pessimistic in observing that they offer a gloomy picture indeed. None of these variables are truly manipulable in the policy relevant sense that they can be altered easily by the conscious actions of officials.[23] This argues for war as being a heavily "systemic" phenomena, built into the status hierarchy of the international system via the major power/minor power dimension and relationships.[24] The continuation of such a status heirarchy, with the existence of major powers will continue to pose problems in terms of the control of war. George Modelski (1972: 58) writes:

> War has been, and still is, preeminently a Great Power activity hence a product of Great Power dominance, not only in global wars but also in the majority of national and sub-national armed conflicts of the past few decades. Control of war is control of Great Power activity and of the diplomatic networks within which war occurs; it is also the construction of alternative social networks.

The unavoidable factor of international boundaries, of the "we-they" phenomenon of inter-group tension, rivalry, and hostility (concomitant with the intra-group needs of unity, cohesion, and cooperation) are also systemic. They are built into international relations as they presently exist, and will remain as long as there are independent, "sovereign" units, and a continuing history of wars and therefore war coalitions. Hanson and Russett (1972: 17) write in summarizing the research presented in *Peace, War and Numbers*:

> Together, all the papers do produce an image of heavy environmental constraint on nations' behavior, of the serious degree to which nations' leaders are prisoners of the situations in which they find themselves, and especially of their past policies. This emphasis on the structural properties of national systems, the global international system, and of conflict sub-systems should sober us. . . It will be hard not only for policy makers to take new actions but also for peace researchers to identify those variables which are in fact fairly manipulable and thus make possible choices which will break the chain to violence.

A second gloomy note closely related to the first also emerges. Norman Alcock (1972: 197-212) in developing a "dynamic theory of war" connects the arms race phenomenon to the systemic (that is the relational and interdependent) nature of international behavior. The occurrence of "arms races," in this environmental setting, is used to account for the cyclic nature of patterns of international violence. It appears that only a small amount of war or violence with the system at any one point may be enough to keep the various war cycles and processes in motion. It would appear that even 13.5% of all possible war coalition dyads is a large enough number—that even given the non-belligerent nature of the great majority of war coalition partner dyads, 13.5% for the reasons discussed, manage to become Enemies in future wars.

There are, however, a few hopeful signs. Two indicators of bonds of community and ideology were entered fairly high up in the step-wise discriminant function analysis. The cooperative and pacificatory nature of such variables has been verified. It is nothing new to advocate that national decision makers should strive to strengthen such bonds. This may not be a hopeless task. Richardson's idea that the cooperative effects decline over time was verified. This does mean that there is a period of time, for many types of dyads, within which community building activities may take place.

There is very little one can do about Lastwars, wars that have already taken place. However, decision-makers should be made aware of any factors which have been shown to have effects related to war proneness. They can then take extra care in relations with others so as not to exacerbate the factors of belligerency which could, if unattended, truly make them "prisoners of the situations in which they find themsleves." The same could be said of the effects of a common border. In regard to the distribution of spoils, the effects of disparate distribution provide a lesson for how one should treat allies, not only in war situations, but in coalition situations in general. One of the lessons of the earlier study concerned the treatment of war coalition partners. The results presented above confirm the conclusions drawn in theat earlier investigation into war coalitions.

A quantitative investigation of the problems of men and nations is necessarily embedded in the assumptions underlying the "scientific" study of behavior. One such assumption is the development of theory. Although some of the adherents of this approach in the social sciences envisage deductive theory at some future date, others are of the opinion that the most reasonable result will be some form of probabilistic theory. For the study of war, I have interpreted the goal as being a highly sophisticated, complex, multivariate, probabilistic theory of the correlates and causes of war. In terms of an analogy, probabilistic theory acts as an analytic "cookie cutter," delineating the basic shape of those influences and factors impinging on the phenomenon under study. Such theory tells us what conditions will most probably influence the phenomena in question, and the most probable directions of that influence. Just as important, it tells us what influences will be *least* important under certain conditions. As the cookie cutter stamps out a particular shape it also excludes large sections of dough. In the same way, probabilistic theory helps to exclude the least probable alternatives and factors relevant to a particular study. This is what the Sprouts have termed "negative prediction" (1969: 52).

Within a broader context of international cooperation and conflict including the consequences of war, the present paper has investigated a single aspect of the myriad causes and correlates of war. It has looked at the cooperative experience of nations fighting together in war coalitions and asked what effect this might have on war behavior in the future. Several relationships were discovered and explicated. Let us not, however, claim too much in terms of either scholarly advance or policy relevance. Let us merely reshape and modify one small portion of the edge of a very large cookie cutter.

NOTES

1. See, for example: Starr (1974); Singer (1972) or Singer and Small (1972). Other significant manifestations of this trend may be found in the Russett collection (1972), Norman Alcock's summary of research findings (1972), along with numerous conference papers and journal articles.

2. To repeat, we are concerned here with the war coalition experience and not simply the war experience. This research will be dealing with the interplay of war and coalition. What the effects may be of merely being at war or merely being in a coalition are interesting and important questions. However, they are questions to be addressed in later research, and are *not* those with which we are presently concerned.

3. See Starr (1972: chap. 1, appendices A, C). See also Appendix I of this paper.

4. Singer and Small (1972: 19-24; 27-30) provide the data for determining the make-up of the international system at the time of each war coalition. One final note on Non-Participant dyads. Care need be taken in only one matter—that no dyad be counted more than once. For example, Britain appears in the very first coalition in the study, The Greek Revolt. At that time Sweden was a bona fide member of the international system. From the end of that war until the present Britain and Sweden have *never* participated in the same war together. (Which is simple enough, as Sweden never engaged in war during this entire time period.) Thus, the Britain/Sweden dyad is labelled "NI" (never involved). However, Britain shows up in many other war coalitions, and Sweden is a constant member of the international system. For each of these cases, *no* dyad is reported, for to do so would only be repeating the "never" which is stated in the original "NI" coding. Similarly, every Non-Participant dyad had to be carefully checked to make sure that the coding—be it Allies, Enemies or "NI"—was never counted twice for the same event.

5. See Appendix II for a brief description of the statistics used in this paper.

6. See Bishir and Drewes (1970: chap. 20) for a discussion of Markov chains. On p. 615 they state: "Our assumptions are simple. Each trial is assumed to depend on

the immediately preceding trial, when the results of that trial are known, not on any more remote trial." For examples of how Markov models have been used to predict levels of conflict on the basis of previous conflict see, Wilkenfeld and Zinnes (1973), and Wilkenfeld (1972).

7. Here we are testing to see if there is a statistically meaningful difference between two proportions, using Z-scores to indicate whether or not we should accept the *null* hypothesis that there is no difference in the proportions of Allies and Enemies found in War Coalition Participant dyads, as compared to the proportions of Allies and Enemies found in Belligerent dyads. In all cases we can reject the null hypothesis. For example, comparing the proportion of 't+k' Allies resulting from War Coalition Participant dyads to the proportion of Allies resulting from Belligerent dyads, we can reject the null hypothesis that there is no difference on the basis of Z = 5.4. The probability level associated with this value indicates that we would expect to have such a comparison of proportions when the null hypothesis was true, once in 10,000 times. See Blalock (1960: 176-179).

8. There is one question that might be raised about the analysis which has just concluded. Some might ask: is it fair to look at the future from the point of a war coalition whose dyads have, say, 140 years of future to become involved, and also from the point of view of the last coalition, that of the Arabs in 1967, whose members have only five years to get into war before this study's arbitrary cut-off date of 1972? Admittedly, there might be some sort of time threshold operating within which it might be very difficult for a nation to become involved again with former war coalition partners. But, this seems doubtful. It appears quite easy to get into war again within a short period. For our 297 involved dyads, 126 or 42.4%, become involved again with former war coalition partners *within* five years. It would appear that this inequity in temporal opportunity to become involved—while a possible distortion—does not seem to be operative.

9. For example, see Wright (1965) chaps. 35 and 36, and appendices 40 and 41. See also, Wright (1969), Rummel (1965; 1971), and McClelland (1971).

10. In the earlier study, the characteristics of the war, including length, were derived from the data sets of Wright, Richardson, and Singer and Small. Data agreed upon by two of the sources in distinction from the third was used, with heavy reliance on Singer and Small after World War II. See Starr (1972: 9).

11. See Richardson (1960: 4-10), and Starr (1972: Appendix I).

12. Using 1913 as a cut-off point instead of 1900 would result in the switching of only 18 't+k' involved dyads from the later time period to the earlier one. Sixteen of these dyads are derived from the two Balkan wars. These wars, integral to the pre-World War I period, appear to be more sensibly grouped into the same period as the First World War, as indeed they are in the pre-1900/post-1900 time split used in this study.

13. This "feudal" conception of the international system is diagrammed by Jenkins (1971: 83) as follows:

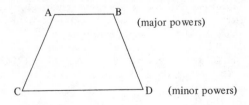

where a short line indicates greater interaction than a long line. Note that AC or BD is still shorter (more interaction) than CD.

14.

	OneSpoils		OneTerritory		OneIndemnity	
	x^2	p	x^2	p	x^2	p
Whole Sample	.41	.52	.005	.94	.38	.54
19th Century	.61	.43	.04	.83	.92	.34
20th Century	1.43	.23	.02	.90	.035	.85
Over 25	.13	.72	.17	.72	2.46	.12
0-5 Years	.42	.49	.03	.86	.003	.96
Minor Powers	2.58	.11*	1.04	.31	2.57	.11*

*wrong direction;
hypothesis disconfirmed

15. An identical hypothesis was tested using indemnity rather than territory. As indicated in Table 8 this was not confirmed. There was no general relationship using difference of means (t = .68) or correlation (r = −.05). *No* relationships were discovered for either century nor for groups based on Major Power/Minor. Only the Under 25 group shows a weak tendency to confirm (r = −.13, p = .07). This perhaps indicates the weak effect indemnity has in terms of forestalling the emergence of Enemies in the short run.

16. The final hypothesis proposed that greater disparity in scores indicating general goal fulfillment would be related to a greater probability of dyads becoming Enemies. This was not supported for the whole sample (t = .028; r = −.002) nor for any of the subgroups. For a further discussion of this variable, see Starr (1972: chap. 9).

17. The importance of the short-term future, as a dominant focus in international relations is discussed by Burns (1968).

18. However, a number of the independent variables are also dichotomous, some nominal, some ordinal, some interval. There are questions as to whether certain types of independent variables may be used in certain types of multivariate statistical techniques. Sanford Labovitz (1967; 1970) has presented some strong arguments allowing for the use of such variables in multivariate techniques like discriminant function analysis. For further discussion and references, see also, Bohrnstedt and Carter (1971), and Suits (1957).

19. The program used here was Biomed, BMD7M, Stepwise Discriminant Analysis. See Dixon (1970: 214a ff.).

20. When Share of Territory Difference is entered, the F values for the other spoils variables plummet, as this variable takes up or explains the same or more variance as these other indicators. The F values of the others behave in the following fashion:

Unfairness of Territory Distribution	drops from	6.50 to	.07
BothSpoils		1.99	1.34
BothNotIndemnity		2.95	.75
BothTerritory		3.95	2.50
BothNotTerritory		4.03	.21
BothIndemnity		2.40	1.13

21. GINI Indemnity discriminates between Enemy and Allied dyads in that Allied dyads show certain relationships with GINI Indemnity, while Enemy dyads show none at all. Therefore, while this variable does discriminate between the two groups, it is not very helpful in providing us with information about Enemy dyads.

22. The final results, which include the minor effects of 18 additional variables, add only 8.8% more cases correctly grouped.

23. See Raymond Tanter's discussion (1972) of policy relevance criteria and his focus on manipulability (control) or research results. See also Burgess and Lawton's (1972: 71-76) discussion of the need for "design theory," with additional references.

24. A literature concerning the international sociology of hierarchy and status has been developed and augmented with a variety of works such as: Galtung (1964), Lagos (1963), Heintz (1972), Wallace (1972; 1973), and East (1972).

REFERENCES

ALCOCK, N. Z. (1972) The War Disease. Ontario: CPRI Press.

ALKER, H. (1965) Mathematics and Politics. New York: Macmillan.

BARRINGER, R. E. (1972) War, Patterns of Conflict. Cambridge: MIT Press.

BISHIR, J. W. and D. W. DREWES (1970) Mathematics in the Behavioral and Social Sciences. New York: Harcourt, Brace & World.

BLALOCK, H. M. (1960) Social Statistics. New York: McGraw-Hill.

BOHRNSTEDT, G. W. and T. M. CARTER (1971) "Robustness in regression analysis," pp. 118-146 in H. L. Costner [ed.] Sociological Methodology. San Francisco: Jossey-Bass.

BURGESS, P. M. and J. A. ROBINSON (1969) "Alliances and the theory of collective action: a simulation of coalition processes." Midwest J. of Political Science 13: 194-218.

——— and R. W. LAWTON (1972) Indicators of International Behavior: An Assessment of Events Data Research. Beverly Hills: Sage.

BURNS, A. L. (1968) Of Powers and Their Politics. Englewood Cliffs, N.J.: Prentice-Hall.

CARROLL, B. A. (1969) "How wars end: analysis of some current hypotheses." J. Peace Research 4: 295-322.

COBB, R. W. and C. ELDER (1970) International Community, A Regional and Global Study. New York: Holt, Rinehart & Winston.

DENTON, F. H. (1966) "Some regularities in international conflict, 1820-1949." Background 1966, 4: 283-296.

——— and W. PHILLIPS (1968) "Some patterns in the history of violence." J. of Conflict Resolution 12: 182-195.

DEUTSCH, K. W. (1964) "Quincy Wright's contribution to the study of war," pp. xi-xvii in Q. Wright, A Study of War (abr. ed.). Chicago: U. of Chicago Press.

———, et. al. (1957) Political Community in the North Atlantic Area. Princeton: Princeton U. Press.

DIXON, W. J. [ed.] (1970) BMD, Biomedical Computer Programs. Berkeley: U. of California Press.

EAST, M. A. (1972) "Status discrepancy and violence in the international system: an empirical analysis," pp. 299-319 in J. N. Rosenau, V. Davis, M. A. East [eds.] The Analysis of International Politics. New York: Free Press.

GALTUNG, J. (1964) "A structural theory of aggression." J. of Peace Research 2: 95-119.

HANSON, B. C. and B. M. RUSSETT (1972) "Introduction," pp. 9-17 in B. M. Russett (ed.) Peace, War, and Numbers. Beverly Hills: Sage.

HEINTZ, P. [ed.] (1972) A Macrosociological Theory of Societal Systems With a Special Reference to the International System. Bern, Switzerland: Hans Huber.

JENCKS, H. W. (1973) "The great powers and war: 1902-1971." Paper prepared for the Peace Science Society (Western) Conference, San Francisco, Feb. 1973.

JENKINS, R. (1971) Exploitation. London: Paladin.

KORNBERG, A. and R. C. FRASURE (1971) "Policy differences in British parliamentary parties." Amer. Polit. Sci. Rev. 65: 694-703.

LABOVITZ, S. (1967) "Some observations on measurement and statistics." Social Forces 46, 2: 151-160.

––– (1970) "The assignment of numbers to rank order categories." Amer. Soc. Rev. 35: 515-524.

LAGOS, G. (1963) International Stratification and Underdeveloped Countries. Chapel Hill: U. of North Carolina Press.

McCLELLAND, C. A. (1971) "Field theory and system theory in international relations," pp. 371-385 in A. Lepawsky, E. H. Buehrig, H. D. Lasswell [eds.] The Search for World Order. New York: Appleton-Century-Crofts.

––– and G. D. HOGGARD (1969) "Conflict patterns in the interactions among nations," pp. 711-724 in J. N. Rosenau [ed.] International Politics and Foreign Policy. New York: Free Press.

MODELSKI, G. (1972) "War and the great powers." Peace Research Society, papers 8: 45-59.

PRUITT, D. G. and R. C. SNYDER [eds.] (1969) Theory and Research on the Causes of War. Englewood Cliffs: Prentice-Hall.

RAI, K. B. and J. C. BLYDENBURGH (1973) Political Science Statistics. Boston: Holbrook Press.

RICHARDSON, L. F. (1960) The Statistics of Deadly Quarrels. Chicago: Quadrangle.

RUMMEL, R. J. (1965) "A social field theory of foreign conflict behavior." Peace Research Society, Papers 4: 131-150.

––– (1971) "A status field theory of international relations, Research Report No. 50, Dimensionality of Nations Project. University of Hawaii.

RUSSETT, B. M. (1963) Community and Contention: Britain and America in the Twentieth Century. Cambridge: MIT Press.

––– (1965) Trends in World Politics. New York: Macmillian.

––– [ed.] (1972) Peace, War, and Numbers. Beverly Hills: Sage.

SINGER, J. D. (1972) "The 'correlates of war' project: interim report and rationale." World Politics 24: 243-270.

––– and M. SMALL (1966a) "Formal alliances, 1815-1939: a quantitative description." J. of Peace Research 1: 1-32.

––– (1966b) "National alliance commitments and war involvement, 1815-1945." Peace Research Society, Papers 5: 109-140.

––– (1968) "Alliance aggregation and the onset of war, 1815-1945," pp. 247-286 in J. D. Singer [ed.] Quantitative International Politics. New York: Free Press.

––– (1972) The Wages of War 1816-1965. New York: Wiley.

SKJELSBAEK, K. (1971) "Shared memberships in intergovernmental organizations and dyadic war, 1865-1964," pp. 31-61 in E. H. Fedder [ed.] The United Nations: Problems and Prospects. St. Louis: Center for International Studies.

SPROUT, H. and M. (1969) "Environmental factors in the study of international politics," pp. 41-56 in J. N. Rosenau [ed.] International Politics and Foreign Policy, rev. ed. New York: Free Press.

STARR, H. (1972) War Coalitions: The Distribution of Payoffs and Losses. Lexington: D.C. Heath.

——— (1974) "An appraisal of the substantive findings of the correlates of war project." Paper prepared for International Studies Assn. Meeting, St. Louis, March 1974.

SUITS, D. (1957) "The use of dummy variables in regression equations." J. of the American Statistical Assn. 52: 548-551.

SULLIVAN, J. D. (1972) "Cooperating to conflict: sources of informal alignments," pp. 115-138 in B. M. Russett [ed.] Peace, War and Numbers. Beverly Hills: Sage.

TANTER, R. (1972) "The policy relevance of models in world politics." J. of Conflict Resolution 16: 556-583.

WALLACE, M. D. (1972) "Status, formal organizations, and arms levels as factors leading to the onset of war, 1820-1964," pp. 49-69 in B. M. Russett [ed.] Peace, War, and Numbers. Beverly Hills: Sage.

——— (1973) War and Rank Among Nations. Lexington: D.C. Heath.

WEEDE, E. (1970) "Conflict behavior of nation-states." J. of Peace Research 7: 229-235.

WILKENFELD, J. (1972) "Models for the analysis of foreign conflict behavior of states," pp. 275-298 in B. M. Russett [ed.] Peace, War, and Numbers. Beverly Hills: Sage.

——— and D. ZINNES (1973) "A linkage model of domestic conflict behavior," pp. 325-356 in J. Wilkenfeld [ed.] Conflict Behavior and Linkage Politics. New York: David McKay.

WOLFERS, A. (1962) Discord and Collaboration. Baltimore: Johns Hopkins Press.

WRIGHT, Q. (1965) A Study of War, abr. ed. Chicago: Univ. of Chicago Press.

——— (1969) "The form of a discipline of international relations," pp. 442-456 in J. N. Rosenau [ed.] International Politics and Foreign Policy, rev. ed. New York: Free Press.

ZIPF, G. K. (1949) Human Behavior and the Principle of Least Effort. Cambridge: Addison-Wesley.

APPENDIX I
War Coalitions and Dyads

Coalition	Number of 't+k' dyads: Allies	Enemies	NI	Total
Greek Revolt 1821-30: Winning Side	4	2	0	6
Losing Side	0	1	0	1
First War of LaPlata 1825-28	1	0	0	1
Belgium Revolt 1830-33	3	0	0	3
2nd War of LaPlata 1839-52	6	0	4	10
Egyptian War 1839-41	3	0	0	3
Austro-Sardinian War 1848-49	1	0	0	1
Crimean War 1853-56	4	6	0	10
2nd Opium War 1856-60	6	0	0	6
Italian War 1859	1	0	0	1
Mexican Expedition 1861-67: Winning Side	0	1	0	1
Losing Side	3	0	0	3
Spain vs Peru/Chile 1865-66	0	1	0	1
Lopez War 1864-70	0	0	3	3
Schleswig-Holstein 1864	1	0	0	1
Austro-Prussian War 1866: Winning Side	1	0	0	1
Losing Side	6	0	22	28
Franco-Prussian War 1870-71	0	0	6	6
Russo-Turkish War 1876-78	9	6	0	15
War of the Pacific 1879-83	0	0	1	1
Boxer Rebellion 1900	27	19	9	55
Central American War 1906	1	0	0	1
Central American War 1907	0	1	2	3
First Balkan War 1912-13	3	3	0	6

Coalition	Number of 't+k' dyads: Allies	Enemies	NI	Total
Second Balkan War 1913	6	4	0	10
World War I 1914-18: Winning Side	24	21	10	55
Losing Side	6	0	4	10
Russian Intervention 1918-20	6	4	0	10
Riffian War 1921-26	0	0	1	1
World War II 1939-45: Winning Side	67	14	129	210
Losing Side	1	0	20	21
First Arab-Israeli War 1948-49	6	0	4	10
Korean War 1950-53: Winning Side	17	1	102	120
Losing Side	0	0	1	1
Suez 1956	0	0	3	3
Third Arab-Israeli War 1967	0	0	6	6
	213	84	327	624

APPENDIX II. SOME NOTES ON METHODOLOGY

Several different statistics are used in this study. Rai and Blydenburgh (1973: 8) talk of "statistical models," and that:

The role of statistical models is to establish the correspondence between a theory and the "reality" the theory is intended to represent. After the researcher has chosen a cognitive model, translated it into a theory, and tentatively accepted the theory as representing the essence of the phenomenon under observation, he must devise formal tests of propositions drawn from the theory. Statistical models facilitate such tests.

However, there are a great variety of such statistical models. The choice of which statistics to use is often dependent on the kinds of data used to operationalize the propositions under study. In order to move from theoretical concepts to empirically defined ones, the concepts must be operationalized. This decision involves the questions of how concepts are to be measured. There are various levels of measurement as illustrated in the independent variables listed in Table 7. Nominal scales are at the simplest level of measurement, whereby things are labelled and assigned to categories. Type war is an example of a nominal scale. Nextwar is also, as dyads are thrown into one of two boxes, one called Allies the other Enemies. An ordinal scale goes a bit further and ranks or orders the categories in regard to some attribute they possess. Timecode is such an indicator, with categories based on ever further periods of time beyond the war coalition. There are also interval scales (without a natural zero point) and ratio scales (with a natural zero point), both of which have *meaningful* distances between observations. Many of our indicators are based on indexes and can be considered interval, such as Deadliness or Coalition Ideology/Community Score. A ratio scale is a type of interval scale; two examples here are Length of War and Coalition Size. They will be labelled as "interval" in Table 7.

The kinds of data which the independent variables constitute lead us to use certain types of statistics. The predominance of nominal, especially dichotomous, variables helps explain the wide use here of the chi-square, one of the number of statistics that may be used to study the relationship between two or more nominal scales. The chi-square may be used as a test in two basic ways, (see Rai and Blydenburgh, 1973, chap. 7). The first is a goodness of fit test performed on one variable. The purpose here is to test the null hypothesis that observed frequencies of the variable do not differ from some set of expected frequencies. This is the purpose of the chi-square employed in investigating the "chance" hypotheses of Table 6. The second type of test is one of "independence." Here the null hypothesis holds that there is no relationship between two variables, that they are independent of each other. In testing the hypothesis set out in Table 8 we are asking whether or not we can reject the null hypothesis that the occurrence of 't+k' Allies or Enemies is independent from some other variable, such as a common border, the occurrence of a Lastwar, and so forth.

A number of variables involve interval scale data. Given the questions being investigated in the latter part of this study, we need a statistic which will help us decide how Enemies differ from Allies. One way to do this is to determine whether or not the means of the two groups (or samples) are different. For this purpose we use a difference of means t-test to accept or reject the null hypothesis that there is no difference between the means of Allies or Enemies on a given variable, such as Coalition Size or Timespan, (see Blalock 1960: 170-176). The Z-test used for testing differences of proportions in Tables 4 and 5 is employed in a similar manner, as described in note 7. As with the chi-square, higher values allow us to reject the null hypothesis with greater certainty that the value did not come about by chance (and thus that we really should reject the null hypothesis). The degree of certainty is indicated by the probability levels reported.

Finally, with the interval data we also wish to investigate the relationships between variables. The product moment correlation coefficient permits us to see if the values of one variable are systematically related to those of another. It is a measure of association. A coefficient (r) of $+1.00$ or -1.00 means that two variables are perfectly correlated—with high values on one variable associated with high values of the other in the first case, and high values of one associated with low values of the other in the second case. Values approaching zero mean there is no systematic relationship. Additionally, the correlation coefficient when squared (r^2) is used to indicate the amount of variance "explained" by the independent variable as opposed to random factors, (see Rai and Blydenburgh, 1973: 198-199).

Finally, we use a multivariate technique which also will permit us to discover how Enemy dyads differ from Allied ones. The technique employed is discriminant function analysis, and is described briefly in the text.

HARVEY STARR is Assistant Professor of Political Science and Senior Fellow at the Center for International Policy Studies at Indiana University. He earned his masters and doctoral degrees at Yale University. In 1971-1972, he was a Visiting Fellow in Politics at the University of Aberdeen, Scotland. He is author of numerous journal articles, book chapters, and WAR COALITIONS: THE DISTRIBUTION OF PAYOFFS AND LOSSES (1972), Lexington Books.